Unbound Writing

*How to write the transformational book you're
really here to write*

Nicola Humber

ISBN: 978-1-913590-05-5 (paperback)
ISBN: 978-1-913590-06-2 (ebook)

www.theunboundpress.com

Nicola Humber

For Dad

Contents

AN INVITATION TO STEP INTO THE PORTAL...

After writing two transformational books myself, and supporting many other women to do the same, I've become enthralled by the deep and mysterious magic that's activated when we choose to say, 'yes' to ourselves and commit to writing a book.

Of course, we want to inspire change and new perspectives in our readers. But the transformation that happens as an author, both throughout the writing process and by actually releasing your book into the world, is surprisingly potent.

I know I've been blind-sided in the most disruptive and delicious way by some of the changes my books have brought into my life.

Writing a book is like casting a spell; although we can never be completely sure what's going to be unleashed during the process, we choose to do it anyway.

This, unbound one, is a heroine's journey.

Each book has the potential to be a magical portal, a doorway to a new world - both for you and your reader.

Each book has a very specific medicine that it's here to share with us.

And each book gives us the opportunity to alchemise the magnificent imperfection of our experience into gold.

The truth is that anyone can write a book. You might find yourself disagreeing with this right now (and we'll be talking more about this throughout these pages), but we could all get a few thousand words down and put them together in a book.

What fascinates me is what happens when we allow the book-writing process to go deeper, when we say, *'Fuck it!'*, get naked and dive way down beneath the surface, letting go of the shoulds and any need to be acceptable, sensible or approved of.

What fascinates me is what happens when we make ourselves fully available to being transformed by the very act of writing a book.

This is unbound writing. And this is the process we'll be exploring together here together in this book.

When you see book-writing as an alchemical process, when you're willing to be transformed by the process of writing, you make space for your reader to experience the same.

Writing a book can change your life.

It can open you up to experience more of yourself.

It can take you in new directions.

It can call you to embody your work and your message at a deeper level.

And it can put you in the way of unexpected and expansive opportunities.

Believe me, I've experienced ALL of the above through writing my books. And now I invite you to do the same.

Whether you've written a book (or books) already, you're in the process of writing one right now, or you find yourself thinking about the possibility, I want to introduce you to a different, deeper, richer, more magical way of writing.

It's not the faint-hearted, but I've got a feeling you're ready.

Shall we?

UNBOUND WRITING ACTIVATION

*If the book I'm writing (or wanting to write)
were a magical portal, what would it lead to?*

FIRST, A STORY

On a particularly grey day in December 2016 I sat at the dining room table in my home in Southampton, England. I was on a call with my mentor and I was trying to describe how I was feeling.

To be honest it was challenging to find the words. Everything in my life was fine. Earlier that year, I'd published my first book, *Heal Your Inner Good Girl*. My business, helping women to move through money blocks and create an abundant income, was flowing well. And Mr H and I had just accepted the opportunity to relocate to upstate New York.

But...

'It's like the walls of my house are falling down around me', I explained. 'And I'm just left in this space, this void.'

I kinda cringe reading that now, because it sounds so dramatic. But these are the words that came when I tried to describe what I was experiencing internally.

And as I look back I can see how I was laying the foundations for one of the most transformational (and turbulent!) periods of my life.

My second book had started calling to me not long after *Heal Your Inner Good Girl* had been published. I'd been feeling pretty darn pleased with myself.

I'd done it! I'd written a book. It's something I'd always wanted to do, and although I knew I'd write more books, I didn't think the next one would come through so quickly.

But here she was calling, another book that was pushing me to start LONG before I felt ready. And all I knew about this book was that it would be called *UNBOUND*.

So I started. Because I've learned through hard experience that when I don't listen to these calls, they just keep getting louder and more uncomfortable.

And writing *UNBOUND* led me to trust the great unfolding of life in deeper, more profound ways than I'd ever done before.

This book came to me in snippets, small and juicy chunks of messy magic that usually left me quite breathless and wanting more. But it became clear that *UNBOUND* would come through in her own time and in her own, unique way.

This was no linear, straightforward process. I'd feel inspired to write about themes that seemed completely unrelated.

It's about sex!

No, it's about shadow work.

Hang on, maybe it's about living in your gift?

What's this about sisterhood?

Nothing seemed to fit together. Each of the pieces that I wrote felt powerful, but was this ever going to be part of a coherent whole?

I'd go for weeks without writing anything and worry that this book was never going to get completed. And then I'd feel inspired again and start writing ferociously.

Throughout this time my life was going through upheaval after upheaval. I'd completely lost any sense of direction in my business. Mr H and I were navigating the challenges that come with relocating to another country. We spent months at a time apart, as he moved over to the States before me and this led to us feeling disconnected and questioning whether we even wanted to stay married. There were serious health challenges within my close family.

It.

Was.

A.

Mess.

But fortunately I'd created a powerful container for myself. I'd made a strong commitment to my book, even though writing it could feel like I was in the middle of a wild sandstorm. And I'd stepped into a transformational mentoring process that gave me the space to explore and be with whatever was coming up.

So I trusted.

And by the end of the year, the sands had finally settled. I saw that UNBOUND had started to take form. When I looked at everything I'd written, I could see how it would fit together. It felt like magic!

And what I was left with was not just a book, but a complete shift in direction.

Throughout the year I'd been working on UNBOUND, my mentor (who is incredibly intuitive) kept getting the message that I was going to be helping women to write books. 'I can see you running writing classes', she'd say, after one of our deep-diving sessions.

'Hmmm', I'd say, thinking that there was NO way I could help anyone else to write when my own process was so, well, unbound.

But when I delivered the final manuscript to my publisher, Sean Patrick of That Guy's House, and met with him in London to discuss the launch plans, he too had a vision for me. 'You know, I can see you running your own publishing imprint and helping other women to write books like this. It would be called something like The Unbound Press.'

As soon as Sean said those words, I felt a deep sense of knowing, a kind of remembering, in my body. I had no idea how, but I knew that this was what I was meant to be doing.

And so UNBOUND has kept calling me to start before I'm ready and to learn through doing.

When I started to run the first round of the Unbound Writing Mastermind in August 2018, I knew that I could hold a super-potent space for anyone who joined, but I was quick to say to the women joining, 'I'm not a book coach, so this is going to be an experimental, evolving process.'

And somehow, magic happened. Because I'd been through such a transformational writing process myself, I could help the members of the Mastermind in times when it felt hard to find their way, times when they were in the void and not wanting to write at all, times when they were feeling called to share something that felt risky or vulnerable in their writing. And the books that came out of this process have been stunning.

In November 2018, I launched The Unbound Press, a soul-led publishing imprint for female writers whose work activates transformation in other women. Again, a part of me was saying, 'What the fuck are you doing Nic? You don't know anything about publishing!'

But my Unbound Self KNEW that this was what I was meant to be doing. I allowed myself to be supported as I found my way and when our first book was released in April 2019, The New Normal by Jennifer Booker, I cried tears of joy and gratitude.

What a wild ride! Writing UNBOUND was a portal for me to move more deeply into who I am and what I'm here to do in the world. And that book birthed an incredible platform through which other women can share their unique medicine. The magic keeps rippling out!

And the reason I'm sharing this with you as we begin this journey together, is that if you're thinking about writing a book, or you're in the midst of writing one right now, I know it can feel scary. You might be questioning yourself continually and faced with unexpected challenges along the way. But please know, what you're creating in the world, what you're going to create, IS needed. It's needed for you and for each of the readers who will be impacted by your book.

So stick with it, unbound one. Because you never know what your writing will birth! And I, for one, can't wait to find out.

UNBOUND WRITING ACTIVATION

Think back to a time within the past five years that has felt like a turning point for you. What felt challenging for you then, how did you move through it, and what's unfolded since?

OVER TO YOU: THE CALLING

I wonder why you picked up this book (or downloaded the electronic version)? What ignited your curiosity to discover more about writing a book? What has brought you to this point?

It could be that you're not even sure yourself, but I have a pretty clear idea.

You've been called.

You see, you've always been a writer and it's likely that this idea to write a book has been buzzing around for quite some time - months or maybe years. Can you think back to when this desire to write a book first surfaced? Perhaps it feels like it's always been there?

Maybe....

You've been feeling the call to write a book ever since you were a child? I know that was the case for me. Little Nicola always loved reading books and writing. I wanted to be a writer - that was my dream. And then I lost touch with that calling for a big part of my life when I was following the good girl path, getting my education, working in finance in a corporate environment and doing my nine to five. When I started my business, it started to call to me again, this desire to write a book, but I'd lost that sense of possibility, that dream that I could be a writer. I certainly didn't see myself as creative. And it took quite a long time for that to come back for me.

Maybe you've been guided to write a book? Perhaps the angels, your Higher Self, or some other intuitive guides have been telling you to write your book? I hear this from a lot of women. And this was the case for me when I wrote my first book, Heal Your Inner Good Girl. It had been bubbling away for a long time when I had an angel reading and the first message that came through was *'Have you written your book yet? You need to write your book'*. Maybe you've had a similar reading or that guidance is coming through in some other way. Please know, if you're receiving this kind of guidance, it's no accident. It's important that you take action on that and move forward with writing your book.

Perhaps you started to write a book and got stuck somewhere in the process. Once again I know this is the case for a lot of people (and it's certainly applied to me!) I started to write my first book many, many times before I actually fully committed to it, because these myths I'm about to share with you were keeping me stuck. And I know it's a deeply frustrating place to be when you're half in and half out of your writing process.

Or maybe you've actually written a book already and if that's the case, go you! But you're feeling called to write something that fully expresses the truest essence of who you are. That's what I'm interested in. I'm not interested in you writing any book, (although it's a big achievement to write any book), but I want you to write the book that you're REALLY here to write at this time; the book that fully expresses the deep magic of who you are, because that is the one that's going to have the most powerful effect on you, on your readers and the world.

Side Note:

As you read that last line you might be thinking, 'Oh, my book's not going to change the world'. But let me tell you, unbound one, every time a woman shares her story and her magic, and commits to that fully, it changes the world. That's why our vision at The Unbound Press is to change the world one book at a time. This is not just a marketing phrase. This is the impact we can have when we write these kinds of books.

A year before I started The Unbound Press, when I had NO idea I would be starting a publishing imprint or doing this kind of work, I connected with a powerful vision during a session with my mentor.

I saw myself with a group of women around me, each one carrying a drop of silver liquid. One after another, each of the women stepped forward with her droplet and together they formed a beautiful, silver pool.

As I connected with that vision, I knew that as well as being beautiful, that silver pool was so powerful it could move mountains; that when combined, the magic that each of these women carried was potent enough to be world-changing.

And although at that time, I had no clue how that vision would manifest, I can now see that this was setting the scene for The Unbound Press and the work we're doing there. Each silver drop is a book and when they come together, we have the power to move mountains, change the world and birth New Earth.

Whatever has brought you to these pages, I want you to know...

'If it comes through you, it's for you'.

Do you believe that? All of those unexplained desires, dreams and ideas that pop up seemingly randomly and out of the ether, can they all really be for you? Even the outrageously abundant, unusual or out-of-character ones?

Yes!

If you've felt the call to write a book, if the idea has arisen for you, it's no accident.

Whatever you might tell yourself, this is not a case of mistaken identity. Oh no.

If it comes through you, it's for YOU.

Yes, my love, you are a writer. And yes, there is a very specific book that is longing to come through you.

So are you going to keep it waiting?

Of course, it's one thing to hear the calling and notice that tug of desire. It's quite another to actually trust it and move forward from that place.

Self-trust; in truth this is all that's required to write a book (or create anything in your life).

Self-trust is listening to those breadcrumbs of inspiration and allowing yourself to follow them, even if you don't have the whole path mapped out. (In fact, ESPECIALLY if you don't have the whole path mapped out).

But the thing is, from a very early age, we're taught NOT to trust ourselves. We're conditioned to continually look outside for the answers - to our parents, our teachers, the church, the media - anywhere but inside.

As women, we're taught to not trust our bodies; they're wrong, dirty, too big, too small, too hairy, too smelly, too unruly.

We receive the message that we're too emotional, too complicated, too much (and not enough at the same time).

In the patriarchal system we currently live within, hierarchy is everything and so we're taught to always be looking out and up towards someone who 'knows better', trying to find an expert, a guru.

Well here's a spoiler alert for you: no-one knows you better than you.

No-one knows your path better than you.

No-one knows your unique magic better than you.

And no-one knows what's for you better than you.

So, what if you chose to actually believe that? To anchor into your inner knowing and trust yourself beyond all else.

What if you chose to simply notice any questions or doubts that come up when the insight of an idea arises for you and move forward anyway?

But what if I'm making it up?

My first step on the unbound path was to train as a hypnotherapist. When I had my hypnotherapy practice and I was leading clients through some kind of guided visualisation process, a question that often came up was: 'What if I'm just making this up?'

What if this isn't actually coming from my subconscious or collective consciousness?

What if I'm just wishing this into my mind?

And this may well come up for you during the unbound writing process. What if this isn't actual inspiration? What if I'm making this up?

My answer to this is: So what?

Even if you are 'making it up', isn't it interesting that you're making this specific 'thing' up at this time? It's always coming from somewhere and out of all the limitless ideas, words, insights that could be coming through you right now, this is the one that's coming.

To me, that's a miracle. Every single time.

So, rather than closing yourself down and telling yourself to 'be more realistic', choose to be curious about your wishes.

Listen to those seemingly random thoughts that pop into your head.

Each word you express is a gift. And this expression can be both sacred and playful.

Just let it come, unbound one.

I invite you to see this whole process as an experiment in self-trust. You've already felt the calling, so it's time to say, 'Yes!'

Allow yourself to be available.

Practice receptivity and willingness.

You can't get this wrong.

Can you feel the freedom of that?

UNBOUND WRITING ACTIVATION

What is wanting to be expressed through me right now?

WHAT IS UNBOUND WRITING?

Well, thank you for asking, magical one. Although it's not especially easy to put into words. Let me try though as I want to give you a sense of this path you're stepping onto...

Unbound writing is to write from your Unbound Self, the fullest, freest YOU, who has no inclination to hold back, edit herself or dim her light.

Unbound writing is to write freely, without hesitation or pausing to wonder whether others will approve of what you're expressing.

Unbound writing is to go to your edges, to invoke the parts of you that have been judged (by yourself and others) as 'too much' or 'not enough'.

Unbound writing is to acknowledge and harness your cyclical nature as you create.

Unbound writing is a way to channel the voice of your soul onto the page, giving her a place to play and experiment.

Unbound writing is a way of connecting with and activating others through what you express. It creates both challenge and deep understanding of self and others.

Unbound writing is sitting with the discomfort of not having a clear plan or structure. You make a commitment to allowing what wants to emerge,

emerge and recognise that clarity comes through allowing your words to flow onto the page.

How does that feel to you?

As I wrote the above definitions of unbound writing, I noticed myself getting excited about the potential of words. How these symbols on the page enable us to communicate ideas, to share understanding, to create healing, to inspire and entertain.

How one word can have many meanings and each of us can perceive that meaning in exquisitely different ways.

How the act of writing these symbols onto the page can free something up within us, allowing us to access new levels of insight and inspiration.

Writing surely is a magical process.

And when you share your writing, you share the magic. You share YOUR magic.

But so many hold back in their writing; either writing in a half-hearted, trying-to-be-approved-of way or not getting started at all.

Hiding.

Their.

Light.

And.

Their.

Glorious.

Shadows.

Why? Because of the countless messages we receive about how we 'should' be.

Because only certain, specially appointed people can be writers, right?

Because you've been made to feel too much and not enough all at the same time and what the freak do you do with that? Well for one, you feel paralysed creatively.

Because your creative energy, your life force, has been stifled, numbed, depressed.

So as we begin this journey, I want you to know that unbound writing is different.

Unbound writing has no rules.

You can't get it wrong.

And actually, when you feel you've got it wrong, you are SO deliciously right.

Unbound writing turns the old ways on their heads.

Unbound writing doesn't aim to get a specific, defined reaction.

Unbound writing is free. And spacious. And furtive. And potent. And fierce.

The very act of writing turns YOU on.

Everyone has a story to tell. And it's not about the number of words you write or the amount of books you sell. It's about deep connection. Deep creativity.

The underlying principle

The most important aspect of unbound writing is that it's a transformative process.

Unbound writing is alchemical. You transform as you write and your writing creates transformation in others.

This is the principle that lies underneath everything else we'll be exploring in this book. And this is the principle that enables you to write in a way that makes the most powerful impact.

Making yourself available to being transformed through your writing can feel challenging. It means that you have to be willing to go to your edges. If you want to write a book that has impact on other people, you have to be impacted by the very process of writing it. Otherwise, your words will feel flat.

Most people would prefer to have a clear idea of what their writing process and book is going to look like when they begin. They'd like to have it all mapped out with chapter headings and a definite structure. And maybe you're looking for that right now? Perhaps that's why you picked up this book?

The truth is that if you have your book all planned out at the beginning, it's not likely to create transformation in you, because when you know exactly where you're going with your writing, you can tend to go into autopilot and revisit the familiar.

When you allow yourself to sit in a place of unknowing and be open to what wants to come through, then that's transformational in itself. And you might be surprised about some of the ideas, themes and insights that come up for you along the way. You might be challenged by what you feel called to write about (and certainly by the idea of sharing it publicly!), but you can know that this is creating transformation for you.

The unbound writer goes first

As an unbound writer, you have to go first. You allow yourself to experience transformation and that creates the space for your reader to be transformed and activated by your writing.

You have to have a meaningful experience through your writing. So, when I see offerings like 'Write a book in a weekend' or something similar, I know that it's not likely to be transformational. The unbound writing process needs time.

Time to access different levels of yourself.

Time to tune into what you want to express.

Time to recognise what's coming up for you around your writing and to experience the challenge of it.

If you just rush through the writing process, then these awarenesses are not going to happen.

On going slow

One of the things I particularly love about the book-writing process is the invitation to go slow. Yes, we could rush our writing, we could choose to get our books done quickly, but there's something about the book-writing journey that encourages a slower pace.

In this world that seems to speed up, moment by moment, where we're consumed with the need for immediate gratification, the slowness of creating a book can feel like a long, delicious breath out.

You can take your time here. In fact, taking your time will only add to the process.

Each of my books has invited me to go more slowly.

Heal Your Inner Good Girl was written over six months, *UNBOUND* took more than a year and *Unbound Writing* has meandered into a glorious twenty months.

And this process hasn't always looked like writing.

When we take our time, we get to live our books, and allow our books to live through us.

New insights and perspectives bubble up and under in the spaces between our writing.

And although the ego may feel impatient with the slow pace - *'Will I EVER get this done?'* - your Unbound Self knows that this is what creates depth, richness, and magic.

Your writing becomes layered with meaning

The energy of presence infuses every word.

Your reader's soul is soothed by the spaciousness of your process.

Going slow is both luxurious and courageous.

The outer world will tempt you with its need for speed. It's easy to find yourself sucked into the overriding desire for a finished 'product' (and on to the next thing...).

But instead you take a deep, nurturing breath, right down into your belly and sigh:

'Not me. I'm here for the journey. And I choose to be enriched by every beautiful step'.

Get to know your book over time and it will reward you with unexpected magic and the depth of connection you can't create with a quick fling.

Sink into slow.

Allow your body to feel the space you're creating for her and for what wants to come through.

There's no rush here.

The energy of writing

When you allow yourself to be transformed by your writing, it changes the energy of your words. Unbound writing is an energetic process. And this is the same with anything you create and communicate, whether it's making a video, speaking in person at events, or even working one-to-one, people can FEEL what you've experienced. They can pick up on your energy, and they pick up whether you're just going through the motions or whether you're really there with them. Your readers will be able to feel that in your writing. And your book will be deeply compelling to the right people - the people who are just waiting to receive your unique medicine.

This means that your book is not going to appeal to everybody. And the fact is that you don't want it to appeal to everybody, because again, there's likely to be a flatness to it if everyone's response is, 'Oh yeah, it's okay, I don't mind it, it's all right'. You want people to be saying, 'Oh my goodness, it's like you're speaking directly to me in your writing!'. They can feel you through your words and they have an energetic response to the experience of reading your book.

You have to allow yourself to be transformed and challenged through the process in order for your readers to experience that. As I said earlier, unbound writing is an alchemical process. You're transmuting your experience into gold. Everything that comes up around writing your book and sharing it with the world, all the fears, all the doubts, all of these old patterns, you have the opportunity to take those and transform them into the gold of compelling writing that makes an impact.

We'll be diving into this more later in the book, but allow yourself to sit with this for a while.

UNBOUND WRITING ACTIVATION

What is the transformation I'm willing to experience as I write my book?

CLUMSY AND INARTICULATE?

So many people tell me they want to write books, but they're not sure if they can because they don't feel articulate enough.

'My words feel clumsy!'

'Others seem to express themselves much more powerfully than me'.

These are sentiments I've heard over and over again in my years of working with different writers.

And I get it. Completely.

I'm a writer. And sometimes (or should I say, often!) I also find it challenging to find the 'right' words. I can feel clumsy when I want to express myself. Words suddenly feel limiting.

And yet, I write. I've felt the call to write since my earliest years. In fact, I wrote my first 'transformational' book when I was seven years old. It was called The Wise Owl and told the story of a creature who didn't quite fit in and then discovered his true self. But I suppressed this calling for a long time. I chose a more sensible path - a sensible degree in Business Studies, a proper job in finance. I forgot that I always longed to be a writer.

I forgot myself. Until I remembered.

When I started my business back in 2010 as a hypnotherapist and coach, I started to write again. I blogged and shared my thoughts on social media. And although I knew that I wanted to write a book, I could never quite commit fully to it. I would begin and then drift away again.

Easily distracted. Easily pulled away from my calling. Easily pulled away from myself.

It's only when the Universe created some space for me, my business slowing down to a crawl in 2015, that I finally allowed the calling back in. And this started me on a new part of my path, writing books and holding space for others to do the same. I'm sure I'll share morsels of my story in these pages, but for now I want you to know:

If you've ever felt the calling to write a book, even if it was years ago, it's no accident.

If you've ever felt clumsy or inarticulate with your words, you're still a writer.

And if you're not sure where to start, then this is exactly what this book is designed to help you with.

These pages will create a space within you to uncover, discover, unbind, connect with, experiment, explore and play with whatever wants to come through at this time.

And I invite you to simply notice any fears, doubts or 'What ifs?' that come up as we journey together. Notice them and know that they're all a part of the process; your process. *And I'll help you to alchemise these into the gold of compelling writing later on.*

I invite you to be curious, playful and reverent of your own unique magic. *And if you don't believe you're magical, I promise you'll find this within yourself along the way.*

Here's to our clumsy, inarticulate and completely magical selves!

Are you ready, unbound one?

UNBOUND WRITING ACTIVATION

If I gave myself permission to be clumsy and inarticulate, what would I want my reader to know right now?

WHAT THIS BOOK WANTS YOU TO KNOW

I'm sat in bed as the snow falls gently outside in Rochester, upstate New York. It's the 11th of the 11th, 2019 and I'm pondering a question my mentor asked me earlier: 'What if your book has something it wants to tell you about the writing process, or even your way of being? It feels like your book wants to tell you something.'

What a juicy thought! So initially, I took myself out for a walk to connect with whatever wanted to come through, but then it felt much more conducive (and kind) to climb into bed and actually ask the question in writing. After all, that's how my book is used to communicating with me - through words, written on the page. And it feels like the words have been flowing through more easily in bed. What a gorgeous thought - that we can create most powerfully whilst relaxing! Maybe that's what my book wants me (and you) to know?

Let's find out together now. 'Dear book, what do you want me to know?'

Oh, I'm SO glad you asked! And part of it is about creating with kindness. The human race has forgotten this in large part. You can create so compassionately, being deeply kind to yourself and others in the process. The kindness ripples out.

You've been used to operating in tension. But there's a different quality that comes through when you allow yourself to enjoy every part of this. Be free. I'm here to support you always. You're always supported. You only have to ask.

Challenge the norm. Be magnificent. And invite others to do the same. You and your community will create change through writing. It's time. Each book is a piece of the puzzle. Except there is no puzzle. Everything is here. And you rediscover this, you remember this, through writing. I love you.

Well, thank you book! That feels so very powerful. No pushing. Just peace.

How about you?

So, how about you, unbound one? What does your book want you to know?

What new way of being is your book inviting?

What are you being called to rediscover, to remember, through your writing?

There is so much available to you in the writing process. Each book has the potential to activate something greater, deeper, richer, when you allow it to.

In August 2019, I ran the Magical Portal Project, a community project where I invited different authors to share how writing a book changed their lives. In her contribution, Anaiya Sophia, author of *Fierce Feminine Rising*, spoke to how each different book has something specific to share with us as the authors:

'*Try as I would, I was unable to write this book as I did my others. All my usual ways were rendered useless. For a start, I could only hear Her (the Fierce Feminine) in the dark. If my mind was busy with planning, organizing, or sticking to a deadline, She fell silent. Only when I sunk beneath the surface did I find Her. Her voice is there for all of us to hear if only we are willing to silence our own.*

As I was writing, She gave me strict guidelines on how this book was to be transcribed. She called this the "embodiment process". From what I understand, this process, this book, and everything within it, is a living hologram. It is an in the moment experience. She wanted me to write as close to the moment as was humanly possible. I was unable to write anything if it was in the past; I could only write what was alive in the very now moment. She wanted me to write while it was still raw and partially formed, and to trust that. She wanted me to go through this unravelling process and to narrate my experiences. This kept me ever-expanding, reaching for new words and ways to transcribe that which I did not know, and yet, strangely did.'

The message here? Trust yourself as you embark on your book-writing journey. The way you write can be just as important as what you write.

There are so many rules and expectations about the writing process, but they're mostly based on old, limited, patriarchal and hierarchical ways of being.

We're way-finders. And I'm curious about what happens if we allow ourselves to discover new ways of mapmaking through making our maps, through writing our books?

This takes space. And curiosity. And willingness to unlearn and listen to what wants to come through.

Are you willing?

Finding your way

This book offers three main sections to guide you. We'll begin very shortly by busting through five myths that could have been holding you back from writing your book up until now. Then I'll share the five layers of unbound writing that will infuse your book with depth, richness and magic. And finally we'll dance through the four stages of the unbound writing process, so you can anchor into what you need and want to focus on in your writing at any particular time.

You'll also find an Unbound Writing Activation at the end of each chapter (you will have seen the first few already). These take the form of reflective questions that are designed to activate your inner transformational author in the most potent way. Simply reading them is likely to spark something within you, but if you take the time to journal on each one (even for a few minutes), you're sure to uncover some new or forgotten magic that has been trying to find you. Once you have read through this book for the first time, I invite you to revisit it throughout your writing process. You might like to open it randomly at any page and see what guidance is there for you on any particular day. You can dive back into any part of this book and allow it to hold space for your own unique writing journey.

On holding space

And going back to that final sentence of the last paragraph, I want to add something here about how books are able to hold space. You might be familiar with holding space for others and I'm sure you've had the experience of someone holding space for you, either individually or as a member of a group. But a book? Is it really possible for a book to hold space?

Well, yes, I believe it is. This book, your book, any book has the potential to hold space for the reader to enter a different state, to access new insights and awarenesses, to experience a shift of perspective and connect with an expanded sense of possibility. When a book is written with the intention of not simply passing on information, but creating a sense of activation in the reader, then it becomes a powerful space-holder in itself.

My intention with this book is not to tell you step-by-step how to write a transformational book. My intention is that this book will hold space for you to find your own unique way, to access the truest essence of your voice and what you're here to share at this time, to activate a deep sense of purpose within you and to help you move more deeply into your soul work.

I want you to feel held and supported as you go forward on this journey and I trust that this book, which has an essence, a personality, a spirit, all of its own, is able to do that.

When we see books in this way, we don't have to micromanage the reader's experience; we can trust that each person will receive what they need from reading our books. There's a quality of spaciousness in that which feels incredibly freeing - both as the author and the reader.

I wonder what your book is going to hold space for?

UNBOUND WRITING ACTIVATION

What does my book want me to know right now?

A PRAYER FOR THE BEGINNING OF THE UNBOUND WRITING PROCESS

I am ready to begin now.

I choose to commit to this process of writing and sharing the book my soul is calling me to write at this time.

I am free to express myself fully and I celebrate my unique voice.

I infuse my writing with qualities of expansion and evolution.

I trust myself and what wants to flow through me.

I make myself fully available to this process. I allow myself to find my own way, whilst knowing that I am deeply supported, always.

I am an expression of the divine as are my readers and all beings and I am willing for all of my needs to be met as I move through my book-writing process.

I call forward my support team now, both seen and unseen, so that I can embark on this journey in the most powerful and magical way.

I am free, fierce and complete.

I allow myself to express all of the qualities I hold within me.

I embrace my powerful cyclical nature.

I am the writer I am here to be.

And so it is.

THE FIVE MYTHS OF BOOK-WRITING
(and how to make sure they don't get to apply to YOU as an unbound writer)

I know there are many different ways you could share your message, your magic, your unique medicine with the world. But there is something truly magical about books (and I know you can feel it if you're reading this). It's likely you've always loved books and had your nose in one continually when you were little. You realise there's something very special about having a physical book in your hands, the feel of the cover and the paper as you turn the pages. And when you write your own book, you can know that it's going out into the world, getting to live with people in their homes. Your readers have a part of you, a part of your essence with them, sitting on their bookshelves and bedside tables. And we should never underestimate the importance and intimacy of that relationship.

So this is why you've been feeling the call to write a book, unbound one. Even though it might feel a bit old school, it is still one of the most powerful things you can do.

But most people who feel the call to write a book never end up actually writing one. The idea keeps coming through in different ways, but then the doubts bubble up - *'Oh, I'm not sure if I can really do this'*. And sometimes the doubt is disguised as procrastination or distraction - *'Hmmm, maybe I'll just do it later?'* And very often this is due to one or more of the soul-sucking myths that I'm going to be outing and helping you to kick to the curb during the next few chapters.

Each of these myths could be true if you allow them to be, but what I invite you to do instead is to turn them on their heads, shift your perspective and choose to see things differently. Because you ALWAYS have a choice.

So, let me introduce you to the five toxic myths that could have been stopping you from writing a book up until now, because awareness is power. And once you're aware of these, you can choose to move beyond them.

Shall we?

MYTH ONE:
I NEED A BIG AUDIENCE

So the first myth that could be stopping you in your tracks right now is that you need a bigger audience before you even think about writing a book.

Maybe you have some small list syndrome going on, feeling some shame that your email list isn't that big or you've only got a few people following you on social media, so what's the point of writing a book? No-one will want to read it anyway!

Imposter syndrome can come into play here too and the belief that if you don't have a big audience, then who are you to be writing a book?

All of this stuff can start to creep in and stop you from moving forward writing the book that you are 100% meant to write. (And if you don't believe me on that, keep reading and let me believe it for you, okay?)

So, how can we turn this particular myth on its head and move beyond it? Well let's start by acknowledging that writing a book isn't about numbers. Actually let me rephrase that, because it CAN be about numbers if you're purely focused on writing a best-seller. But when you're writing in this unbound way and wanting to activate transformation in yourself and your readers, being driven only by numbers is just going to get in your way.

The truth is that you could have a huge audience, write a book and it not make the impact that you truly desire. And you could have a relatively small audience and your book has a huge impact on each one of the people who reads it; they make big changes based on your writing, rave about the book to their friends and feel inspired to work with you in some way. Which would you rather have?

The key here is about connection over quantity. So the focus is on the way your book and you as the author connect with the audience that you DO have. When you're writing from the truest essence of who you are, you create a sense of deep connection with each of your readers. Your writing has a potent impact and your book gets to have a long lifetime, rather than fizzling out a few months after it's been released.

What I encourage you to aim for in your writing process and beyond is for your book to have a big impact on each of the people who reads it, regardless of the numbers. Your readers will want to come closer, go deeper, with you and your work, because they love your book.

Also, a big part of the unbound writing process is to grow your audience as you write. This means that even if you do have a relatively small audience right now, you have the opportunity to change that as you write. This means that you don't hide yourself away for a year as you're writing your book and then you say 'Ta-da!' and try and grow your audience then. *And you don't desperately try and grow your community before you even start writing either.* You choose to grow your audience as you write. And the magical thing is that the process of writing a book is something that's truly compelling to share with the people you're connected with. They'll love being taken behind-the-scenes and given glimpses of what you're creating. So, this has the potential to draw more people to you (*We'll talk some more about this later in the book where I share the four stages of the unbound writing process*).

Let me add here that if you're wanting to go down the traditional publishing route, then this myth can be true. Traditional publishing companies will generally be looking for writers with a large existing platform before they consider publishing your book. But there are so many other ways to release your book into the world. You can self-publish,you can choose a hybrid publisher like the Unbound Press (*wink*), you can crowdfund your book - it's all about choosing the way that works for you. So don't let numbers be a barrier to you getting started with writing your book and choosing to share it with the world.

UNBOUND WRITING ACTIVATION

Who do I feel called to write for? What kind of person do I want my book to create connection with?

MYTH TWO:
I NEED TO BE CLEAR

Soul-squashing myth number two is that you need to be completely clear about your book and have it all mapped out before you start to write it. This is the idea that you should be able to sit down, write an amazing book proposal, have all of your chapters planned out and know exactly what you're going to be writing about.

Now I know that traditionally this is how people approach writing a book. I was encouraged to do this when I wrote my first book. But the truth is, this idea felt restrictive to me. And (*don't tell anyone*) I've never written a book proposal.

What I've learned through my own writing process and working with many other unbound writers is that it can be incredibly limiting to start out with a super-clear idea of exactly what you're going to put into your book. You want to leave space for magic to happen, because when you commit to writing your book and more specifically, the book that expresses the truest essence of who you are and what you're here to share at this time, you create a powerful energetic container within which it will start to take form. Ideas will begin to come through and you'll have experiences that are meant to feed into the book in some way. You'll make connections with other people who have something to offer in terms of inspiring ideas for your book. You'll remember things from your past that are relevant to what you're writing about. And you get to trust that whatever is coming through is meant for the book. You gain the clarity as you write.

So this is about turning the *'got-to-have-it-all-figured-out'* myth on its head, because if you're trying to stick to some kind of rigid plan as an unbound writer, it's very likely you're going to find that far too limiting and restrictive - *the end result of which is that you get fed up and lose interest.*

You want to give yourself freedom to write about whatever is coming through and for your book idea to evolve. This can feel messy and uncomfortable, because we're conditioned to believe that we must always have a clear plan. But believe me, there is magic in the mess. Through my own process of writing books and holding space for many writers in the Unbound Writing Mastermind, I've seen clarity drop in and ideas evolve in the most unexpected and potent ways right through the book-writing process. Sometimes you might think you're writing one book and you end up with something else completely. You have to allow yourself to trust. When you write in this way, which is such a beautiful practice of self-trust, it becomes a powerfully dynamic process. The experience that you're having during the writing process feeds into your book, you share pieces of your writing as you go, engage with your audience and your potential readers, and the work you do with clients during this time can also inform your writing, making it this super-rich and multi-layered experience. Allow yourself to experience moments of clarity, certainly. But don't let the expectation that you will have a step-by-step plan all laid out at the beginning of your process get in the way of you starting to write your book. See this as an opportunity to connect more deeply with your inner knowing, your Unbound Self, your creative muse and the essence of the book that's wanting to be expressed through you. How exciting is that?

UNBOUND WRITING ACTIVATION

How do I feel about not knowing?
What is my relationship with self-trust?

MYTH THREE:
YOU CAN'T MAKE MONEY FROM WRITING A BOOK

So this is a big one - the myth that you can't make money from writing a book. And again, this can stop you in your tracks, because if it's a choice between spending time and energy on projects that are going to generate cash and focusing on something that isn't going to have much of a financial impact, then it's easy to keep pushing your book-writing dreams to the back of the queue.

The truth is that if you're thinking purely about book sales, then this myth could very well be correct. But by turning it on its head, we start to see a different perspective - that in fact your book can be a source of unlimited potential when it comes to income (now doesn't that feel more juicy?).

There are many opportunities to generate income through your book when you see it as a way of creating a written version of you which gets to go out into the world and do your work for you. Your book can do your marketing for you; it can even do your sales for you. I've had people read one of my books and just know they want to work with me without ever having a sales conversation. Your book is an expression of you and your magic. It helps to create connections with people you haven't met yet and a deeper connection with those you already know.

And when it comes to creating income, you don't have to wait until you've finished your book. You might be thinking that you have to spend all this time working on your book, wait for it to go through the publishing process, and at some point, maybe months or even years down the line, when it's out in the world, you can start to make money from it. But no. Once again, I believe in turning this on its head. Because you can be making money from your book as soon as you make that commitment to writing it. As I mentioned in the last point, as soon as you commit to the process, you create this energetic container, where different ideas and inspiration start to come through. As well as feeding into your book, these can help you create new offerings and start working in a way that is fuelled in the most magical way by what you're writing about.

When you're writing your book, you have the opportunity to make money as you go. When you're sharing pieces of your writing along the way, you get to attract your soul-family clients to you. When I was writing *UNBOUND*, I was attracting clients through the pieces of it I was sharing at least a year before it was anywhere close to being released in the world.

Your book can become the foundation of your business. You have the opportunity to have all kinds of offerings based on what you're sharing in your book - retreats, one to one work, programs, events, workshops, whatever you can imagine.

And there's another myth that ties in with this one - the idea that all of this potential is only generated when the book is released, so you have to gear yourself up for that. But again, this just isn't true (and it can lead to authors feeling exhausted and burned out during their book launch and losing the love for their books). As we've been talking about, you can make money during the writing process. You can create income from as soon as you decide to write your book and also for a long time afterwards. When you're choosing to write in this unbound way, your book will have a legacy, a long lifetime. It's not just about the release day, and then maybe a couple of months afterwards. For years afterwards your book will be going out into the world and bringing people to you.

Also, when you write a book it can lead to unexpected possibilities, for example, speaking opportunities and invitations to collaborate with other people. As I shared earlier, The Unbound Press came to me through my writing. I never expected to launch a publishing imprint, but the opportunity came to me through writing and releasing *UNBOUND*. And now I know that this is my soul work. I've created a thriving business that provides a platform for other authors, as well as creating an abundant income for me and my team. How magical is that!

Everything can open up when you finally say yes to yourself and the book you're here to write. And doing this also increases your confidence in yourself. Your book becomes an anchor into the work you're here to do and helps you to acknowledge and appreciate ALL of the wisdom you have to share. This increases your confidence and activates you (and your readers) to value your work more fully.

UNBOUND WRITING ACTIVATION

*What kind of offerings and opportunities might
my book become the foundation for?*

MYTH FOUR:

IT WILL TAKE TOO MUCH TIME AND ENERGY

So, let's move on to myth number four, that it will take too much time and energy to write a book. This is one that holds a lot of prospective authors back because there are so many different things that we could be focusing on at any one time (and often these are projects that feel like a quicker win). So you might find yourself thinking, 'Writing a book is going to take too much effort. I just haven't got the time to do that right now. Maybe it will wait until next month/next year when I have more time?'

If you're anything like me and many other unbound beings, you're pretty impatient. If I have an idea, I want it to be done now. And there can also be this idea that you have to be chained to your desk every day if you want to be a 'real' writer. 'Get up at 6 in the morning and just push through!'

This perceived need to put hour after punishing hour in is something that I heard a lot about when I first started thinking about writing a book. And to be honest, it put me off doing it for a long time because I would hear all of these authors sharing that they'd spend the whole day at their desks and talking about the process in a way that just didn't sound unbound to me. I knew that I couldn't operate that way.

So I want you to know that you don't need to have a rigid and overly time-consuming writing practice, where you have to be at your desk, writing, whether you feel inspired or not. I'm not saying it's easy to write a book; it is a commitment but you can certainly do it in a way that feels good for you.

One of the things we'll be talking more about throughout this book is that it's important to take your cyclical nature into account as you're writing. And this is something that's generally not acknowledged when people are offering advice about how to write a book. Your creative energy will ebb and flow according to where you are in your own personal cycle, the cycle of the moon and the cycle of the seasons. We don't feel the same every day. We don't feel the same at different points during the day, so this idea that we can show up at our desks regardless and just write and push through - it doesn't tend to work for us as the cyclical beings we truly are. And though you *could* force yourself to do that, believe me, you're not going to do your best, most magical work when you're operating from that place of pushing through rigidly.

I encourage you to write from a place of giving yourself permission to honour your cyclical nature and the ebbs and flows of your creative energy. You may prefer to write in small and mighty chunks of time. You might decide to write for 20 minutes at a time and you could still get your book completed within six months or less. Because when you give yourself permission to write in a way that feels good for you, the words are likely to flow much quicker when you do choose to write.

So this is certainly the case for me. I can't write in long blocks of writing. I have to write in super-small chunks of time. For both *Heal Your Inner Good Girl* and *UNBOUND*, I probably didn't write for longer than an hour at a time. And most of the time I was writing for just thirty minutes or so on different days, at different times when the inspiration was coming through. When we create a clear and committed container for our writing, we're not going to float off and never end up finishing our books. We're fully committed to the process, but we give ourselves permission to write in a way that honours the ebbs and flows of our cyclical creative energy.

Rather than writing little and often, you may prefer to write in intensive sessions. You might like to take yourself on a writing retreat for a week or a couple of weeks and just get it done. If that works best for you, then go ahead and do it! Just know that the book-writing process definitely doesn't have to take a huge amount of time.

The fact is that you may have already written much of your book. When you look back at everything you've written in the past - blog posts, social media posts, workshops and programs - there can be a lot of content there already. That said, I believe it's important for your writing to reflect your current experience and the ideas and inspirations that are coming through for you now (especially in these fast-moving times). But you can absolutely revisit things that you've written already and bring that through in your writing.

Turning this myth on its head is really about giving yourself permission to write in a way that works for you, that feels good for you, and knowing that it really doesn't have to take huge swathes of time. Remember, both of my previous books (and this one) were written in small chunks, so I certainly didn't have to switch off the rest of my life and business whilst I was writing. I've been able to focus on other things and still get the books written. And you can do the same.

UNBOUND WRITING ACTIVATION

How do I like to write? What feels like my ideal writing practice and how can I give myself permission to create my book in this way?

MYTH FIVE:
WRITING IS A SOLITARY PURSUIT

Myth five is the idea that writing is a solitary and lonely pursuit. You might think that you have to tuck yourself away in your office for months or years whilst you write your book, feeling isolated and switching off from those around you. And maybe that appeals to you - it certainly appeals to me at times! But even for those of us who are introverts, it's really important that we have a sense of connection. We want to be connecting with others. We enjoy a sense of engagement and we like our processes to be dynamic. So it can be off-putting to think that you have to hole yourself away, and not be connecting with your people, your community, during the writing process.

The unbound way is (of course!) quite the opposite. I encourage you to create community around your book as you write. Your book can become a hub around which you connect with others. And there are many ways to do this.

When I was writing *UNBOUND*, I hosted a Live Your Gift retreat and invited members of my community. The retreat was based on the principles I was writing about in my book, but I didn't wait until it was out there. So, far from being this a solitary process, writing *UNBOUND*, and creating content and offerings around that, allowed me to connect more deeply with my existing community and invite new people to join me.

Turning this myth on its head is about seeing your writing process as an opportunity to intentionally create deeper connection with others. So maybe you'll choose to interview different people from your community in order to create or inspire material for your book. I did this when I was writing *Heal Your Inner Good Girl* - I created a short survey asking questions about other women's experiences of following the good girl path. This gave me great material for my book AND allowed me to connect with the women in my online community.

Jo Gifford, author of *Brilliance Unboxed* and one of our first The Unbound Press authors, purposely created a mastermind which was based on the ideas she wanted to share in her book as she was writing it.This helped to inspire her writing process and make sure that she was writing in a way that connected with and served her audience. #winwin.

There are many possibilities here. And when we allow this sense of connection through our writing, a sense of community, it becomes a dynamic process that feeds you, your writing and your audience. When you give people the opportunity to be involved in one way or another throughout the writing process, they'll be excited to read your book when it comes out.

This means letting go of another myth: that you have to do it all on your own. This is a belief that many of us carry in many different ways and the truth is no, you really don't. Your writing, your life, can be this gorgeous, collaborative, connected experience, and I believe that's what we're all craving right now.

So absolutely have your alone time, feed your inner-world well, and also know that you *can* have this glorious feeling of connection through your writing.

UNBOUND WRITING ACTIVATION

*How might I create connection with my audience
and community during my writing process?*

THE FIVE LAYERS OF
UNBOUND WRITING
How to infuse your book with depth, richness and magic

We now move onto the five layers of unbound writing. These are a set of ideas that will allow your writing (and your writing practice) to feel rich, multifaceted and distinctly magical.

Each one of these layers is based on one of the five principles of living unbound. These principles unlock the door to the fullest, freest expression of who you're here to be in the world and what you're here to share at this time. Anchoring into these layers will enable you to bring this quality of full expression into both WHAT and HOW you write.

At times over the next few chapters I'll ask you to reflect on specific questions or take a particular action. But mostly, I simply invite you to hold each of these five layers in your awareness as you write; they are very often more about being than doing.

Let's dive in...

LAYER ONE:
ALLOW PLEASURE TO
BE YOUR COMPASS

The first layer of unbound writing is to allow pleasure to be your compass. This is likely to be completely different to the more arduous approach we've been taught at school or in employment. And that's what makes it infinitely more magical!

Rather than seeing your writing practice as something you 'should' do, or something you need to get done in order to serve others, what if you chose to see it as an act of self-love, a way of taking pleasure, something you do for YOU? When I interviewed Leonie Dawson, author of the *My Shining Year* books, for the Magical Portal Project, one of the things that stood out for me was her declaration:

'Spoiler alert. I've never written for anyone else except for me!'

I loved this. Because especially as women, we're often taught to put others first, to think about others needs before our own and to move forwards based on that. When I wrote my first book, I was told something similar (and again when I started my business) - 'you need to focus on what your reader/client/audience wants and create something to meet that'.

But that outside-in approach didn't work for me. I didn't feel lit up when I started looking outside for answers. It felt hard and forced and distinctly un-pleasurable.

What I noticed is that when I gave myself permission to play on the page, to write what felt good for me and to allow that feeling to lead me, not only did I create something that felt wonder-full for me, but others loved it too. #winwin.

The power of allowing pleasure to be your guide is like a secret the patriarchy doesn't want you to know.

But unbound one, your pleasure is your power.

So, let's start there with sensual writing.

Sensual Writing

Definition of sensual: Relating to or involving gratification of the senses and physical, especially sexual, pleasure.

When I was at the beginning of the process of writing this book, one of the intentions I connected with was to invoke a feeling of sensuality. I was surprised that this word came up, so I was curious.

What does it mean to allow the writing process, YOUR writing process, to be sensual?

As I'm a word nerd I looked up 'sensual' in the dictionary and the definition I found was the one given above. I also saw on another online vocabulary resource that there was a warning about using the word, as it could have 'unsavoury' overtones.

Really? This could be a whole other conversation! Just because something can be related to sex, does it have to be unsavoury?

Here's what I mean by sensual writing:

To take pleasure from the very act of writing. (*And as I write that, I notice the feeling of my pen moving across the page. I notice how my body feels as I write and consciously slow down. I breathe more deeply, right down into my belly and exhale through my mouth with a delicious sigh. I rest my feet on the floor and notice the cool of the stone beneath them. I settle my back into my chair and allow myself to be supported, taking more space.*)

We're generally not taught to create in a pleasurable way. At school and at work, we're conditioned to '*get it done*', '*suck it up*', and '*push through*'. Production is not meant to be enjoyable. Hence, if you're enjoying yourself, you're obviously not being productive!

But, what if you could savour and take pleasure from the creative process? What if that's the way it's meant to be done? It's likely that your body is not used to that possibility. Mine certainly wasn't. In the past I've tended to notice in my writing that for my words to flow I need to be hunched over, writing quickly, with tension running through my body. And as I came to write this book, I chose to experiment with a different way. A way that feels good. A way that nourishes me, my body, my senses.

Because, why not? Surely if we can create from tension, we can create much more powerfully from pleasure?

So what would it mean to you to write in a sensual way?

How do you want to feel as you're writing?

What do you want to see, hear, taste, smell?

What would it be like to allow yourself to do that?

What would it take for you to savour your writing process, rather than simply pushing through? How can you give yourself that experience?

When I invited author of *Mummy JoJo UNCUT*, Jojo Fraser to share something about her writing process, she said:

'*Writing my first book felt like a treat. I adored bringing my ideas to life on the page and made space for my intuition to tell me which words would work and have an impact on people.*'

To allow your writing to feel like a treat - how delicious is that? And it's completely possible, unbound one. As I share this approach with other writers, they're often surprised to realise that their writing practice becomes just that: a treat.

And I know you might be thinking, '*What's this about savouring the process Nicola? I'm not worried about how I feel. I just want some ideas on what to write about first!*'

But as with anything in life, if you can allow yourself to be intentional about how you want to feel when writing, this creates a powerful space for the ideas to land within you; you'll be more open and receptive to your muse. So, humour me, okay?

Start with pleasure and everything else will fall into place as you move through the next four layers. And if you need some inspiration on how to make your writing process pleasurable, how about allowing yourself to be inspired by one of my very favourite people and authors, Lisa Lister:

'*I ritualize the shit out of my writing process now... each book has its own energy, so I tune into the energy of the book. Love Your Lady Landscape had a signature song (which was "This Girl Is On Fire" by Alicia Keys) and a signature scent, so every time I sat down to write, I'd play that song and I'd light that candle and then I'd just dive in and I'd write some words really quickly, even if they were shit words, even if they were words that were nothing to do with the book, but I would just think to myself, 'Look at me, I'm a writer. I'm a writer and I'm writing words!' Because writing a book is like trickery. We have to trick ourselves all the time, even people that love the idea of being a writer, into the actual act of writing.*'

— *Interview for the Magical Portal Project, August 2019*

And what better way to trick yourself than consciously allowing the experience to evoke pleasure?

There are all sorts of stories that can get in the way of acknowledging ourselves as writers, as authors. And one of the most toxic is that the creative process has to be arduous, filled with challenge, sacrifice and deprivation.

I'm not saying that writing a book doesn't come with challenges. I'm continually going to be inviting you to go to your edges and allow yourself to go on a transformational journey as you write. But your writing can also flow with ease and playfulness and pleasure.

I encourage you to be open to all possibilities as you write. And really, why limit yourself? The page is one place where you can absolutely give yourself permission to be free. We tend to edit and censor ourselves in so many areas of our lives. So I invite you to allow your soul to play on the page, and allow pleasure to guide you.

How does that feel?

UNBOUND WRITING ACTIVATION

How could I allow pleasure to guide me in my writing process?

LAYER TWO:

ALLOW YOUR CYCLICAL NATURE

The second layer of Unbound Writing is to allow and harness the power of your cyclical nature.

Contrary to much of what we've been taught, we're not designed to live and write in a rigid, linear way, feeling the same, and being able to do things the same way, day in, day out. No! You are a cyclical being and you are being influenced in the most magical way by many different cycles at any one time - your own menstrual cycle (if you have one), the cycle of the moon, the cycle of the seasons and the stage you're at in your life cycle.

What this means is that your creative energies will ebb and flow - some days you'll feel super-inspired and want to write, write, write. Other days you might feel more in planning or editing mode. And other times you might feel completely blank, like there's NOTHING that wants to come through.

It's ALL good, unbound one. The key is not to fight against this and try and force yourself to write when your cyclical nature is telling you to go inwards and just BE.

As unbound writer, Ali Roe, shared about being a member of the Unbound Writing Mastermind:

'A key piece of learning from the unbound process [that] has helped across all areas of my life; that I am a cyclical being. In the past, in all my creative endeavours, this is something that I had fought, resisted and misunderstood and it had often led to me giving up on my projects and dreams. I thought that if I had long fallow periods and times where there was no flow, it meant that I wasn't really cut out for creative work. How differently I manage this aspect of my essential feminine energy now!'

Getting to know your own cyclical nature and how you can begin to write in alignment with this takes time. I don't expect you to have it all figured out immediately (or even in a year's time). All I want you to do right now is to sit with the knowledge that your creative energies do have this cyclical quality, and that you will feel different from day to day, hour to hour, moment to moment even. And that's okay.

Start to pay attention to how you feel differently towards your writing from day to day. You might like to make a quick note in your journal about what you feel drawn to each day.

Give yourself permission to follow your cyclical nature. If you feel fired up to write - go for it.

If you feel like you want to make a plan for your writing and what you want to create around your book - do that.

If you feel like you want to review what you've already written and start editing it - follow that feeling.

As ever, you can't get this wrong. Imagine yourself as an explorer who's getting to know your own, unique cyclical nature. Notice how it feels to allow this aspect of yourself.

This is an ever-evolving process and something I encourage all unbound writers to work with. My dear friend, Caroline Palmy, shared the following when she was talking about her writing process for her first book, *Conversations With Me*:

'I learned that I needed to find my own rhythm, be totally open and go with the flow. I know there are writers out there who can only write when they stick to a set routine - that is wonderful, as long as you do what suits you. I did not write for days and then I sat down and wrote 6 chapters in one go.'

Yes! When we go with these ebbs and flows rather than fighting them, we can create much more powerfully and freely.

And following on from this...

The power of a non-linear approach

One of the things that came close to keeping me permanently stuck when I started writing my first book was the mistaken idea that I should write it in a linear way.

As I've already shared, all of the advice I saw and heard told me that I should come up with a clear plan of what I wanted to include in the book and map that out into different chapters. Someone advised me that I should use my 'signature system' and if I didn't have one, I needed to come up with one.

The trouble is I didn't have anything close to a signature system I used with my clients. I had tried to use one in the past, but it felt restrictive to me. I'd get bored trying to stick to a step-by-step approach and knew that I was much more suited to working with clients in a more intuitive, magical way.

Even now, although you could call the unbound writing process a signature system, it's certainly not linear. In fact, this very book is designed to be a free-flowing guide that you can pick up on any given day, open at any page and let it inspire you.

The idea of writing in a systematic way feels stifling to me. And I know I'm not alone. So many first-time authors never progress beyond the start of their writing process because they think they should write the book from beginning to end.

The creative process doesn't work like that. Ideas drop in randomly, your muse wants to go where she wants to go and often, that is a twisty, turny, backwards and forwards path that doesn't seem to make any sense. And the good news is, it doesn't have to.

Giving yourself permission to write your book in a non-linear way is one of the most freeing things you can do.

Just start. Commit to the process of your writing, create the container for your book to come through and follow wherever it takes you.

This approach takes self-trust and courage. There will be times when you think, 'Is this EVER going to come together?' But believe me, it will.

When I was writing my second book, *UNBOUND*, at times I felt like I was actually writing five different books. The ideas that were coming through seemed so diffused and unrelated. I couldn't see how it would ever form a coherent whole. But somehow I allowed myself to trust the process. And as the months went on, I realised that there were some definite principles which brought the book together; principles that are now infusing the different layers of the Unbound Writing process.

I could never have come up with those principles if I'd sat down at the beginning and tried to plan what I was going to write about. I had to follow my Unbound Self and trust her breadcrumbs of inspiration in order to get to the essence of what I was being called to share at that time. And it ended up being more deeply magical and impactful than I could ever have imagined.

That's what happens when you allow yourself to write in a non-linear way. Somehow you cut through the rational, 'should-y', trying-to-figure-it-out mind chatter and connect with the unique medicine you're here to share.

I see this time and time again with the writers in the Unbound Writing Mastermind and The Unbound Press authors. By trusting what's wanting to come through and following an unbound approach, they end up distilling their unique magic onto the page.

Erica Walther, author of the stunning *Motherhood Meets Me*, said this was the most helpful piece of advice I'd given her at the beginning of her writing process. Her book is primarily a memoir, so you'd imagine it would be relatively easy to write this in a linear way from beginning to end. But no. Erica found this was keeping her stuck and jamming up her writing process. When I encouraged her to write whatever was wanting to come through at any particular time, the words started to flow more freely.

And of course, you can put the individual pieces together in any way you choose eventually. But you don't have to make that decision until you're much further into your writing process.

So, unbound one, how would it feel to give yourself permission to write in this non-linear way?

Allowing yourself not to know

One of the side-effects of writing in this non-linear and cyclical way means there will be times on your writing journey when you will have NO clue what to write and that's okay. It doesn't mean you're not a writer or that you shouldn't even be thinking of writing a book.

It's powerful to sit with any un-knowing. The unbound one knows that in order to know, you first have to not know. And not knowing is one of the most potent parts of the creative cycle. In Gestalt therapy, it's known as The Fertile Void. And when I first heard those words it felt like taking a beautiful sigh of relief. Because this void was one that I'd experienced often. But in the past, I'd always judged myself for being there as though it was some kind of failing.

We're conditioned to skip past this stage and rush ourselves into knowing; to force our creative process in a way that leaves us feeling drained and only half-expressed (at best). And although the void can be an uncomfortable place to be, it's also rich with potential.

Everything comes from this space. But we need to be courageous enough to allow it first.

In this world that demands 24/7 content and information, to allow yourself to dwell in un-knowing is a rebellious act.

What's next? I don't know.

There's so much possibility and compassion in those words.

Allow yourself to bathe in them for a moment now, unbound one.

Allow yourself to say, 'I don't know'. When you do this, you make space for what is wanting to emerge. And it may not happen immediately (in fact, it's very unlikely to do so), but when the next idea pushes it's tendrils up through the soil of your imagination, I guarantee it will be fully aligned and deeply magical.

UNBOUND WRITING ACTIVATION

How do you feel about allowing yourself to write in a cyclical and non-linear way? What would it be like to give yourself permission to follow your ebbs and flows?

LAYER THREE:

ALLOW YOUR WRITING TO TAKE YOU MORE DEEPLY INTO YOUR GIFT

The book writing process for me has got me thinking bigger, wider and deeper than ever before. I have been observing my past, connecting those dots and can now see where the dots may lead for me and for others.

   – Sarah Lloyd, author of Connecting The Dots

The third layer is to see your writing as a way to move more deeply into your gift. It's all too easy to underestimate your own unique magic and the very specific medicine you're here to share with the world. One of the five principles of living unbound is to live your gift and believe me, this is one I've personally struggled with over the years (and I know many other women, in particular, struggle with this too). Because to live my gift, I've first had to recognise and acknowledge that I DO have gifts. For a long time I imagined that only certain, very special people, had been anointed with gifts. And I certainly wasn't one of them.

But this is a lie. Because gifts aren't reserved for 'special' beings. Your very existence is a gift. Your presence, your being-ness, is a gift, even without you doing a thing.

And this gift will be brought through in your writing. In fact, whatever you're writing about, it will become infused with the quality of your unique gift.

The fact is that all of the experiences you've had throughout your life, all of the qualities you hold (even those you've judged as wrong or unacceptable - perhaps especially these!) are a code that will run through whatever you write.

Every word you write has the potential to be encoded with the specific medicine you're here to share with the world.

You.

Are.

The.

Code.

How powerful is that? Can you allow yourself to believe it? No worries if not. It's enough to just sit with that possibility for the time being.

When you write, imagine what you're unlocking in others, what you're allowing them to connect with and unfurl.

When you think about it like this, you'll never question what you're meant to write or whether anyone will appreciate it. You write with a trust that the unique codes only you embody are being passed on.

Way-finding

What I'm sure about is that the unbound writing process is a way of bringing forward new ways into the world. It's a birthing process. And that's exactly why often you won't have a clear sense of what you're writing about. Although some of the themes you may be focusing on in your writing are familiar, your perspective will be completely new.

You are a way-finder.

In these transformative and turbulent times, the old ways are crumbling. In fact, in many cases they're falling away dramatically, like a landslide caused by the torrential rains of change.

And this perpetual sense of change and upheaval can feel terrifying. Because what do you anchor into when you're on continually shifting sands?

You anchor into your own magic, your own wisdom, your own knowing - your gift.

And you write. You write to share what's coming through you, your experiences, your insights, those moments when everything clicks into place (even just for a second) and you see life clearly.

You write to ask questions and explore possible answers.

Because the truth is that the new ways aren't clear right now. We have elements of them, but not the full picture.

Your book has the potential to be a piece of this grand puzzle, unbound one.

And although the content you write is absolutely important, the energy that's infused into your words is just as key.

If you think of it in terms of music, each person has their own note, their own tone, their own chord. On its own, this may not sound powerful. But when you come together with others, as a choir, in harmony, the sound is breathtaking. It's a sound that creates worlds.

So you have to trust the specific piece of the puzzle you've been given.

Are you willing to trust?

The golden thread

Your gift is the golden thread that flows through your life. The golden thread of people, places, experiences and learnings that keep and guide you on your soul path. It's a theme, a chord, an essence, that is uniquely yours. And you most likely won't have the precise words to describe your gift. It's subtle and can seem shape-shifting. And that's okay. You don't have to describe it, you don't have to pitch it or write a sales page for your gift.

You are it.

Even if you did nothing else for the rest of your life, your gift would still be there within you, radiating out into the world. But it really comes alive through engagement, interaction and connection.

Your gift awakens through conversation, through sharing and listening, through witnessing and being witnessed.

Your gift is a dynamic process.

That's why I love the process of writing a book (*and of course, more specifically the unbound approach to book-writing*), because it's a channelled way to play with your unique gift, to explore and share it with the world.

Writing a book is like inviting another into your world, inviting another closer. And as really there are no 'others', we exist as interconnected beings, in reality you're inviting yourself closer.

How delicious is that?

When you allow that golden thread to infuse your writing and guide you through your book-writing process, everything opens up.

You have the opportunity to transmute your life experience into gold.

Now this might sound very grand and maybe you feel a sense of pressure as you read this.

'What Nicola? I have to find this mysterious golden thread and infuse it into my writing???'

Relax, unbound one. There's no searching to be done. There's no trying, no striving, no pushing.

This is a process of allowing. Allowing yourself to trust the golden thread (it's the one that's brought you to this page) and to trust the unique layers of your experience. We'll be diving into what makes *you* the perfect person to write *your* book later on. In the meantime, let's look at one of the elephants that can make its way into the room when we start talking about gifts.

It's all been said before.

Yes. It's true. Whatever message you want to share, whatever idea you have, whatever theme you want to focus on, it's all been said before. Probably many, many times before.

And that's a wonderful thing.

Because rather than having the pressure of trying to come up with something new, you can simply enjoy the freedom of expressing yourself in your own unique way. And don't worry about 'trying to' be unique, you already are, unbound one.

Speaking to someone who came along to one of my Unbound Writing Workshops, she was surprised to notice that when people were sharing about their writing ideas, there were a lot of similarities. And what I loved is that rather than seeing this as a bad thing - 'It's all been said before so what's the point?' - she instead noticed the unique way each person had of expressing a similar idea.

The work I do isn't unique. My message is all about living an unbound life, expressing yourself more fully and writing from that place. Basically my message is about freedom and there's nothing unique about that.

But what is unique is my specific perspective, the lens through which I see this process of unbinding ourselves from the stories about who and how we should be in the world.

And the same will apply to whatever you choose to write about.

Your unique blend of experiences, stories and everything that's got you to where you are now is completely unique.

The way you see life is unique.

The way you combine your words is unique.

So, don't get hung up on creating the new (although you may just stumble across something completely innovative along the way).

Also, know that there are collective themes rising at any one time. So don't be surprised (or feel threatened) if you notice many people talking about similar things at the same time. People need to hear the same message from different voices. Your people need to hear it from YOU.

And finally...

Take up space

This is something I wrote about in my first book, *Heal Your Inner Good Girl*, inspired by the poem of the same name by Vanessa Kissule. And I feel called to return to this theme as I share specifically around writing.

Because when it comes to sharing our truth in this way, there still seems to be a reluctance to take up space in the world. In fact, there's often a deep fear of standing out, rocking the boat or being seen as too much in some way.

And this reluctance to take up space is infectious. We see (or sense) other women holding back and follow suit.

So what if your writing could be a way of showing others that it's okay, in fact it's vital, to take up space?

What if you gave yourself permission to stop holding back and decided to go to your edges in your writing?

One of the writing prompts we use in the Unbound Writing Mastermind is allowing yourself to be 'too much' on the page. Very often we've picked up the message that we're too much in some way.

Too loud.

Too bossy.

Too joyful.

Too naughty.

Too angry.

Too sexy.

Too emotional.

Too opinionated.

My invitation to you is to celebrate your 'too much-ness'. Rather than trying to rein it in or mask yourself in a cloak of acceptability, consciously choose to be 'too much' as you write.

This can absolutely start as an experiment. You don't have to show it to anyone. Although you'll probably want to at some point, because what you write from the too-much place is likely to be super potent.

In truth, whenever you're questioning whether you're too much, you're simply expressing yourself fully. And that can take a bit of getting used to when we're conditioned to fit in.

Your gift lies in your too-muchness, unbound one. So let's bring that through in your writing.

UNBOUND WRITING ACTIVATION

Rather than shying away from your 'too-muchness', give yourself permission to bring this quality through in your writing. To experiment with this, take some time and consciously allow yourself to write in a way that feels 'too much'.

LAYER FOUR:
ALLOW YOUR WRITING TO HOLD THE QUALITY OF SISTERHOOD

The fourth layer that you can anchor into during your unbound writing journey is sisterhood. In *UNBOUND*, I talk about how the unbound one thrives in sisterhood, in community. But so often we've received the message that we should be able to do 'it' (whether that's writing a book, running a business, or any other creation) alone.

But you really don't. Writing a book can be tough. There will be times when you feel like giving up. For sure.

So, allow yourself to be supported.

Find an accountability buddy, go to a writing group, hire a writing coach or join a mastermind (ahem, like mine).

When I was writing my first book, *Heal Your Inner Good Girl*, I arranged to have weekly Skype calls with a friend who was also working on a book. We would check-in on how we were doing, share any challenges that were coming up and set intentions for the coming week. Having someone I was accountable to was incredibly helpful. It would have been all too easy to drift away from my writing process if I hadn't known I was going to have these weekly check-ins.

As I was coming to the end of writing this book (which is NOT my favourite part of the writing process), I had daily check-ins with my biz bestie, Tonia G, who was in the finishing stages of her book as well. We used the super-simple (and powerful) tool of Spring Cleaning which we learnt from Mama Gena at the School of Womanly Arts (Google Mama Gena and Spring Cleaning to find out more). These short daily calls were invaluable for both of us; sharing and allowing ourselves to be witnessed in whatever was coming up helped to clear our energy and keep us focused on actually completing our books (the evidence of which you now have in your hands!).

The lesson here is that you COULD do this alone, unbound one. But when you allow yourself to connect with at least one other unbound writing sister who is on the same journey, your book becomes infused with this beautiful energy of support and connection. And you're able to access different aspects of yourself and new insights that will feed your writing.

The sister wound

In *UNBOUND* I talk about the resistance we can often feel to being in community with other women and the beliefs that lie beneath that resistance. Many of us are carrying the sister wound in some way - a deep fear of sisterhood.

Maybe you've felt judged, betrayed, criticised, bullied or misunderstood by other women in the past?

When you allow yourself to be vulnerable and step forward to write in community, a wonderful side-effect is that you're often able to uncover and move through any old fears and patterns that have stopped you connecting fully with others in the past. You have the opportunity to relearn how to be in sisterhood.

For me this has been one of the most magical elements of holding space for groups of women writers. I always knew that creating within a container of group support was powerful - we can gain so much learning, inspiration and activation from those we surround ourselves with. But the shifts that happen around sisterhood were unexpected and potent.

Alison Roe, founder of Ali Roe Creative, shared the following after attending a Magical Portal Writing Retreat with a small group of women who were all part of the Unbound Writing Mastermind:

'I would say that the most beneficial aspect of the retreat was the opportunity to sit in circle with unbound women. This experience showed me how I have unbound from some old beliefs, behaviours and patterns and where I am still stuck or bound. Stuck, sometimes, in the spiral of lessons still needing to be learned – particularly about myself in relationship to others' judgement and approval and in owning my true unbound identity fully and fearlessly. I have never before witnessed and been part of a group of women who have so courageously, openly, honestly and unashamedly shared their vulnerability and their truth.'

The truth is, when we try and write on our own, it can feel tempting to jump ship when the process becomes challenging. You might tell yourself, 'Oh I was never really that serious about writing a book anyway. I can always come back to it another time.' When you're writing within a group, the qualities of accountability, shared intention and belonging carry you through.

As Jessy Paston, author of Release the Wild Within shares:

'Being part of the Unbound Writing Mastermind has been the most transformative and healing process I have ever been through. The aim was to get my book written, which is coming along nicely, but being part of the writing group was much, much more. So many laughs, tears, acceptance and encouragement.

The writing process is a powerful one but can be quite a rollercoaster. I had tried to write on my own but have done so much more being part of this group. This has been a magical experience for me - a true gift to be able to connect with soul sisters, especially in these uncertain times.'

Your support team

So how can you allow yourself to be supported and access the magic of sisterhood? Maybe you have a friend who's also writing a book? Perhaps you could join or create a writing circle (or come join us in the Unbound Writing Mastermind?).

However you choose to move forward with this, I can't tell you how very powerful it is to have a community of other writers around you. People you can say, 'I've got nothing this week' to. People who will say, 'Oh my goodness, I've been feeling like that too!'

People who will see you sharing a piece of your writing online and cheer you on.

People to inspire you and people you inspire.

The magic flows in all directions.

But we're conditioned to believe that we shouldn't need support, that we should be able to do it on our own.

That is the way of separation. Isolation.

And separation and isolation don't create a strong enough container for creativity.

Unbound one, you deserve to be supported.

You deserve to be held.

You are doing a great service to the world with your writing.

Allow yourself to be held in that.

Allow the essence of sisterhood (or brotherhood or community if you prefer) to be infused into your process and your readers will feel that deep sense of connection and holding.

UNBOUND WRITING ACTIVATION

How do you feel about sisterhood? What would it be like to allow yourself to be beautifully supported throughout your writing process? What would that support look like?

LAYER FIVE:

ALLOW YOUR WRITING TO ALCHEMISE YOUR SHADOW

The fifth layer of unbound writing is to see the whole process of writing a book as a powerful opportunity for shadow integration. What do I mean by this? Well rather than hiding, repressing, forgetting or ignoring the parts of us that we've judged to be unacceptable, shameful, icky, weird or just plain wrong in the past, we instead welcome them into our writing.

But why on earth would you do that?

I know. It sounds scary to share that 'stuff' that we've been doing our best to keep in the shadows up until now. And isn't writing a book about showing your most shiny, expert, 'look at how amazing I am!' self?

Well you can certainly approach it in that way if you choose. But what creates REAL connection with your reader is when you allow your full self to be seen (and that doesn't just mean your shiny bits).

Let me elaborate. One of the things that can hold us back in our writing is a fear of how others will react. Something rises up within us that we want to share, we feel a sense of excitement, and then...

The doubts bubble up.

What if someone gets angry about this?

What if I get judged?

What if I upset a friend or family member?

What if I attract criticism?

Ebonie Allard, author of *Misfit to Maven*, shared about her experience of this during the Magical Portal Community Project:

'*Writing a book is always an exercise in commitment, conviction and self belief. Writing an incredibly personal and reflective piece about the journey you went on (to the darkest parts of yourself) requires an even deeper connection to something bigger than you...*

Publishing it even though I was scared to was my initiation. In the moment that I chose my message, my people and giving them the book I knew that they needed even though it terrified me, I became a Maven.'

It's all too easy to get tangled up in the 'what ifs?' and promptly swallow our inspirations back down. And the problem here is that not only do the people who need to hear our words not get to receive them, but the swallowing down of our expression can negatively impact us.

We can feel heavy, sluggish, rigid and incomplete, carrying our ideas inside us, not allowing what desperately wants to be expressed to move through us.

We feel blocked.

The Sadness

One evening as I was writing this book I checked in with my guides during a meditation to ask, 'What's the most powerful thing for me to share right now?'

The answer came swift and clear and simple: sadness.

And although I was surprised, I immediately knew the sadness they were referring to. It's a sadness I lived with for much of my adult life.

A sadness that sits in the belly, weighing you down and making it hard to surface each morning.

A sadness that dulls your eyes and keeps you subtly disconnected from even those closest to you.

A sadness that hangs like a grey fog, blocking you from life's deepest joy and richest experiences.

This is the sadness of not being fully expressed in the world.

The sadness of holding back and stuffing your creative ideas, impulses and inspirations into a dark cupboard marked, 'not for me'.

The sadness of following a path that's not yours, a path that's based on the perceived expectations of others, a path that's paved with countless 'shoulds'.

The sadness that looks like 'my life is great' from the outside, but leaves you feeling dead inside.

Ah yes, THAT sadness.

It's one that can be hard to recognise, acknowledge and share. Because in the scheme of things, in these challenging and turbulent times, is being fully expressed and allowing your creativity to flow REALLY that important?

Well, unbound one, yes it is.

We are all creative beings. And, even if your first thought is, 'no, not me', when we don't allow that part of us to be expressed in the world, something inside us shrivels up, hardens, becomes stagnant and heavy.

Most people are living with this sadness without being aware of it.

This sadness has become normal, something that just is.

But when you allow even one creative idea, impulse or inspiration to flow through you,

When you give voice to your soul in some way,

Something comes alive.

You free up energy, things start to move and your world, THE world responds.

You can feel it immediately. Long forgotten, ignored and suppressed parts of you awaken.

You feel more whole, more grounded in the world, stronger.

You start to experience more moments of pure joy and connection.

And when you are sad or angry or lost, you can see the beauty in that too.

You are.

And the Universe is cheering you on.

So, if you're feeling that sadness right now, or it's familiar to you, take a moment now.

Feel the sadness as a sensation in your body. Give it space. Acknowledge its presence.

And let this part of you know you're willing to express something new in the world.

Something brave.

Something you.

But what if I piss someone off?

Okay, so you're choosing to be brave and express from your heart. You're choosing to invite your true magic out of the shadows. But how do you move beyond the fear of triggering a negative reaction in someone else?

Well, the first step is to acknowledge that we really have no control over how someone else responds to us. Full stop.

Whether you share your magic freely or not, other people could still get pissed at you. And in fact, it can often make it more likely that you trigger a reaction in someone because as the energetic beings we are, people can sense when you're holding something back.

So, why not allow yourself to experience the liberation of sharing your truth?

The second step is a practice. And that practice is one of getting comfortable (or more comfortable) with being with people who are experiencing strong emotions. You have to be willing to invoke strong reactions in others. In fact, as a writer, that's kinda what you're here to do.

Now I know this isn't easy. Believe me, this has been one of the biggest challenges for me as I've walked the unbound path. For most of my life I had a deep-seated fear of making others angry. I would remove myself from any situation where it felt like conflict was about to rear its head. I just couldn't be with strong, seemingly negative, emotions.

But this kept me in a constant state of self-monitoring.

Is it okay to say this?

What will they think of me?

What if they don't get it?

And I kept quiet most of the time. I was detached; detached from others, detached from life and detached from my true self.

And you know, unbound one, that's no way to live.

So, this has been a journey of allowing myself to be with anger, sadness, misunderstanding, judgement, criticism and ridicule. Sounds fun, doesn't it?

But really, when you boil it down to its essence, what we're really afraid of when we think about evoking a particular reaction in someone else is the physical sensation that this creates within us.

What happens in that moment when you realise that someone is angry/disappointed, just not getting you?

You simply feel a sensation in your body.

Maybe it's a sinking in your stomach, a constriction in your throat or a tightness in your chest (or perhaps all of this). But it's all about sensation.

I know that this can be intensely uncomfortable. In fact, we'll do pretty much anything to avoid these physical sensations. So much so that we're willing to put up with feeling numb most of the time.

But if you're not willing to experience moments of intense discomfort (eurgh! That person is really angry with me right now), then it's likely you're also not fully available to moments of intense joy and pleasure. You can't numb to one thing without numbing to everything to at least some degree.

So, let's come back to those fears now.

Ask yourself, what's the worst that could happen?

Yes, you might make someone angry, sad, confused, disappointed. And you might experience the physical sensations that accompany being with that response. But you'll survive. And more than likely, this full expression will lead you to thrive.

Now, as I say that, I recognise I'm writing this from a place of privilege as a white, cis, hetero, able-bodied woman. I know that not everyone experiences the safety to express themselves fully. Many people in the world risk physical danger, imprisonment or even death for speaking and living their truth.

As Jennifer Booker, author of *The New Normal: Coming Out as Transgender in Mid-Life*, shared about writing her book:

'*[It was a] relief that I got to tell my story before anything happened to me. As a transgender woman who refuses to hide in a closet, I recognize that it is risky to be so public, especially under the current political climate in the United States. Writing gave me peace of mind that I got to leave a legacy through my book.*'

So, if you're reading this and it feels risky to think about expressing yourself by writing a book, please know that I see you. Take your time with this, get the support you need and please do feel free to reach out to me directly. Your words are important and I will do everything I can to help you find a way to share them.

On the other hand, if you know that your only risk is the discomfort of someone being pissed off with you or not fully getting you, then isn't it worth the risk?

Our stories matter

'*I don't know if I really want to write this book*'.

This is a statement that one of the women shared on the final morning of a Magical Portal Writing Retreat I was running. And I completely understood her point. There are many ways we can express ourselves - social media, videos, blogs and podcasts and articles.

Why would you need/want to write a book?

Because our stories matter. So many women over thousands of years have had their stories twisted, dishonoured and censored.

So many voices have been silenced, cut-off, shut down.

Women's stories are quite simply missing from much of the HIStory we're taught.

And still many women, many people, are unable to tell their stories. It's not safe for them. Many would literally risk their lives if they chose to express themselves fully.

But we can.

It will be scary and challenging. We may feel clumsy or self-indulgent. We may risk criticism or ridicule.

But we have the freedom to tell our stories.

And we have a duty to do that. A duty to all those who've been silenced, hidden, censored.

A duty to our ancestors and those yet to come.

A duty to ourselves.

Which leads me to...

The boring truth about 'Who do you think you are?

There's one thing I can pretty much guarantee for you when you start writing a book.

That it will be hard work? Nope.

That it will be a best-seller? Well, fingers crossed but there's no guarantee.

The one thing I CAN guarantee is that you'll have at least one instance of thinking, 'Who do I think I am writing a book?'

And I'll wager that this will be followed by some (if not all) of the following thoughts:

'Who would want to read what I have to write?'

'I'm not a good enough writer'.

And, 'Maybe I should put this to one side and go back to tidying my sock drawer/scrolling through Instagram/watching Netflix' (*delete as appropriate*).

These kinds of thoughts are so all-prevailing that it almost becomes boring.

I was speaking with a client recently who had just been through a panic about actually releasing her book and she said, 'But I know it must be normal, right? Because you write about it all the time. Why do you think we have this?'

Great question! Because I've experienced these doubts (over and over again). The writers I work with in the Unbound Writing Mastermind experience these doubts (I mean, I'm good, but working with me doesn't dissolve all fear and doubt. I hold a pretty fierce space to move beyond them though!). And the most well-known, best-selling authors in the world experience them too.

So, why? Well from a very early age we receive countless conscious and unconscious messages that we're not good enough, that we should pipe down, be quiet, hold back and make ourselves acceptable/approved of/liked.

So, when we start to think about writing a book, all the ways we've been told to get back in our box bubble to the surface.

Added to that, very often we're carrying the idea that writing a book is only for 'special people' - and goddess forbid that you should think of yourself as special!

So, the idea of putting your head over the parapet and actually writing a book is just too much.

But when we recognise how prevalent these fears and doubts are, how much they're a part of our current human experience, we can choose to move beyond them.

Just because you have the 'who do I think I am?' doubt, it doesn't mean you're:

Unworthy

Deluded

Not cut out to be a writer

It simply means you're choosing to move more deeply into your unique gifts and towards the parts of you that have been dwelling in the shadows. So, go you!

I used to share a whole load of techniques to release these kinds of limiting beliefs and stories: Emotional Freedom Technique (EFT), hypnosis, journalling, visualisation.

But honestly? The most powerful technique I know is to recognise the complete mundanity of these doubts.

I mean, yawn!

So my invitation to you whenever a, 'who do I think I am? Obviously I'm not a good enough writer' thought pops into your head is to think, 'Oh you again! I must be on the right track'. And keep write on (see what I did there?) with your amazing and much-needed book.

I'll be giving you a potent way to reframe the 'who am I to?' question whenever it comes up during the writing process. But in the meantime, I want you to simply know:

Your fears and doubts, what lies in your shadow, the parts you resist, hide and have tried so hard to forget, are your superpowers. Allowing yourself to be vulnerable and invite them into your writing process will create deep connections - both with yourself and your readers.

Know that you probably won't feel amazing, energised and focused throughout the writing process. I know it feels great at the beginning, but writing a book is like anything else. Some days you'll feel blank, some days lost, some days sick and some days pissed off. #truthtalk.

Disheartened, frustrated, angry, sad, anxious, fearful... Shall I go on?

I'm not saying this to freak you out. I'm simply being honest. You are a magical, unbound being and that means you experience the full spectrum of emotions. Just because you're writing a book doesn't make any difference to this I'm afraid.

But this is good news. Because as we've been talking about in this chapter, you don't just want to write from your happy, shiny place. That's all well and good, but your reader will want you to hold space for ALL of them. And that means writing from it all.

Allow your lost-ness, your confusion, your rage, your sadness, your fear, your grief, to have a voice.

All of these emotions, these aspects of you, have something to express, to share. So rather than making yourself wrong and thinking, 'I'm obviously not meant to be doing this if I'm feeling this way', allow your feelings to enrich your writing.

This is transmutation. Transmuting your experience into the gold of compelling writing.

Are you willing to play in the shadows, unbound one?

UNBOUND WRITING ACTIVATION

Be brave and allow yourself to write about something you've been fearful of showing. You don't have to share this with anyone else (unless you want to!). Just practice writing from the shadows to see how this feels.

THE UNBOUND WRITING PROCESS

So, unbound one, hopefully by now you've got pretty darn clear on the fact that you are here to write at least one book... *Who are we kidding? We both know that even if you haven't started the first one yet, there's a whole procession of magical books just waiting to be birthed through you!*

We've talked about the soul-sucking myths that might have been holding you back up until now and I've introduced some new perspectives to help you turn these on their heads.

And I've shared the five layers of unbound writing that will infuse your words and your process with depth, richness and magic.

How are you feeling?

If you've been playing along with the Unbound Writing Activations I've been giving you, then I'm guessing you've already got some powerful insights into what wants to flow through you and into your book. It might still feel messy at the moment and that's okay. In fact, it's more than okay. The mess is usually where the magic is (if you can allow yourself to sit with it).

Next we're going to be diving into the four stages of unbound writing. Now, this is not some neat and tidy, step-by-step process (*you'd be surprised if it was, I'm sure*). The truth is that you will ebb and flow between each of these stages throughout your book-writing journey. But it's super-helpful to get to know them in order, so you can recognise which stage is going to be most beneficial for you at any one time. So, that's exactly what we're going to do now.

Are you ready?

STAGE ONE: *Commit*

'*Until one is committed, there is hesitancy, the chance to draw back, always ineffectiveness. Concerning all acts of initiative and creation, there is one elementary truth, the ignorance of which kills countless ideas and splendid plans: that the moment one definitely commits oneself, then providence moves too.*

All sorts of things occur to help one that would never otherwise have occurred. A whole stream of events issues from the decision, raising in one's favour all manner of unforeseen incidents, meetings and material assistance which no man could have dreamed would have come his way. Whatever you can do or dream you can, begin it. Boldness has genius, power and magic in it. Begin it now.'

William Hutchinson Murray

Oh my goddess, I love this quote so much. Don't you?

I've included it here at the beginning of the unbound writing process, because it encapsulates the importance of this first stage. And in reality, this is the most vital stage of all. Because if you don't make a commitment, you might still be able to write some kind of book, but it won't be THE book; it won't be that specific, compelling and magical book that's waiting to come through you right now (*and, as you know, that's the book I'm interested in helping you write*).

You, unbound one, need to commit in order for everything wise old Billy shares above to happen, for providence to move too, for the Universe to start moving in your favour. You need to make a clear and true commitment to your writing; and specifically to writing the book that you're really here to write at this time.

This stage removes any of the woolly *'will I or won't I?'* energy and creates a powerful container for your book to unfold. When I made the decision to write my first book, *Heal Your Inner Good Girl*, before I had any idea what it would be about or what it would be called, I started by making a super-clear commitment to the process. And I knew I had to do this, because I'd started many times before, but drifted off to other projects and shiny objects. This time I wanted it to be different. This time I needed it to be different. Because my inner author was tired of waiting.

So I finally decided, *'Yes! I'm going to do this'*. And the sense of commitment was so clear. I could feel it in my bones.

I didn't have a clue exactly what I was going to write about, I just knew that, yes, this was the time. And within a week of making that decision, I was out for a walk, and the title, *Heal Your Inner Good Girl*, came through. The words came to me as a download. And it was crystal clear because providence had started to move in my favour. The Universe had responded to my commitment and said, *'Yep, Nicola's ready now, she's made this commitment, so let's give her the title'*. And from that point I was able to tune into the kind of things that I would be writing about in the book.

And, of course, the book evolved over the time I was writing it. But this is the power of making a really clear commitment to your writing process. Your book will start to communicate with you and you'll begin to get all sorts of ideas coming through. *Please know that this happens in different ways for different people. Some, like me, have the title very early on in the process. Others receive more ideas about the content and the title lands later on and sometimes right at the end of writing.*

Declaring yourself a writer

So how do you make this commitment? Well there are different layers to this. The first part is making an internal declaration; it's making that commitment to yourself, *'Yes! I'm choosing to do this'*.

Perhaps you could do that right now? Take a moment and say to yourself, either out loud or silently, *'I am committing to write my book NOW'*. Notice how that feels. What happens in your body when you say these words to yourself? Maybe you feel a sense of expansion, a tingling, a remembering of who you truly are? What emotions bubble up? Excitement? Anticipation? Fear? Joy? Simply notice what you experience as you make this commitment.

Although I'm inviting you to make an initial commitment now, the truth is you'll be recommitting to your book, to your writing practice, over and over again.

With each of these stages I'm sharing here, you'll move backwards and forwards between them. They're not designed to be linear; there's a cyclical nature to them and you get to spiral round and experience them at different times and from different perspectives. So although you're making this first commitment now *(or very soon!)*, you'll be recommitting regularly as you show up for your writing process.

As another layer of this process of committing to the book you're here to write at this time, I also invite you to make a public declaration about your writing.

This could take a few different forms:

- Share with a friend or family member that you've started to write a book.

- Share a post on social media about your writing plans.

- Introduce yourself as a writer when you meet someone new.

- Write a blog or send an email to your audience letting people know that you're writing a book.

I realise this might feel scary and, most likely, you don't feel ready for this. *The truth is you probably never will and the only way past this is simply to do it.* Know that you can't get this wrong. Whatever form it takes, sharing about your writing publicly will send a powerful message to yourself and out into The Universe that you're fully committed to your book.

If you're sharing on social media, I'd LOVE you to tag me in to your post, so I can cheer you on and follow your writing journey. I'm @nicolahumber on Instagram and @Nicola Humber on Facebook.

Inhabit your being

This stage also involves choosing to inhabit your being as a writer, someone who has something of value to share, the author of the book you're here to write.

Now, as you read that, you may question whether you truly DO have something of value to share. Don't worry - this kind of thinking is very natural, so simply allow yourself to notice it. I'll be sharing a way to alchemise these fears and doubts later on.

So, what do I mean by inhabiting your being as a writer? This is all about embodiment, and how we choose to do this will be unique to each of us. What does it mean for you to embody your being a writer? It's very likely to include prioritising your writing and having a regular writing practice. Maybe it's letting people know that you're writing a book and describing yourself as an author? This can be a big piece - claiming the fact that you ARE a writer.

How do you feel about saying or writing the words: 'I'm a writer' or 'I'm an author'? I know when I invite the women I work with in the Unbound Writing Mastermind or Unbound Book Lab to do this, they can find it challenging. The ego can start to be quite vocal when you begin to shift your identity in this way. *'Really? You're a writer, are you? Well, how can you say that if you haven't even produced anything yet?'*

Imposter syndrome, feeling like a fraud and that you're going to get *'found out'* if you describe yourself as a writer, or worrying that others will think you're getting *'too big for your boots'* if you say you're an author - this is all par for the course. And the only way out is through, unbound one.

Owning the fact that you're a writer is a practice. More than likely it won't come naturally at first. And no-one else is going to magically give you permission to start calling yourself a writer and an author; you have to give YOURSELF that permission. So, start now. The next time you have to introduce yourself to someone, say you're a writer. Include the fact that you're an author in your bio. Play with this. Say the words and notice how you feel in your body. The more you do this, the more comfortable it will become..

Self-care and support

For me, inhabiting my being as a writer means having daily time in nature and prioritising my self-care. Although these are not directly related to my writing practice, both of these elements support me as a creative being and allow me to fill my well before coming to the page.

This part of the process also involves deciding what support to put in place, because as we've spoken about, writing can feel like a lonely activity if you choose to do it completely on your own. So, it's really important to have some kind of support in place. It may be one person that you choose to talk about your writing with, or it may be a group of people where you're able to share, not even necessarily your writing, but what's coming up for you in the process.

Here are some questions to help you feel into the specifics of what inhabiting your being more fully as a writer means to you:

What do you want to put in place to support your writing?

How do you make space for yourself as a writer?

How do you talk about yourself, both internally and to others, when you inhabit your being as a writer?

What do you need to do to prioritise your writing right now?

What opportunities do you seek out as a writer?

What do you choose to let go of to make space for your writing?

Once you've finished, notice how you feel. Is there anything here that you feel resistance around? Again, simply choose to notice this. Write down anything that comes up for you and move on to the next step.

Crossing the Threshold

As we move on from this first stage of the process (for now), I'm inviting you to cross the threshold and firm up your commitment to writing your book.

The truth is that it's all too easy to stay in a place of 'thinking about' writing a book. When you're in this place your writing keeps getting pushed to the bottom of the to-do list, leaving you feeling creatively frustrated and dissatisfied.

As we've been talking about, when you make this clear commitment to writing your book, you create a powerful and magical container within which your book will start to take form; ideas will flow, opportunities will present themselves and you'll feel a sense of devotion to your writing practice.

As we come to the end of this chapter, I want you to imagine that you're crossing that threshold from merely 'thinking about' becoming an author (where your book is only a vague possibility) to actually BEING an author.

This is crossing the threshold from dreamer to writer. Energetically when you do this, you enter a new landscape. You move into a land that is full of possibility and also potential challenges. And as you do this, you will begin to feel different.

You harness a new momentum and enlist seen and unseen guides who will support you in your journey.

Your sense of commitment deepens.

And magic unfolds.

This is a process I guide writers through as a visualisation in both the Unbound Book Lab and at the beginning of the Unbound Writing Mastermind. I invite them to imagine crossing a bridge from one place to another, leaving behind anything that has prevented them from writing their book in the past and moving into a new land where they get to become the writer they're here to be.

So, why not do that now? Imagine you're stepping over from one place to another, from thinking about, to doing. What does the place you're leaving behind look like? What does the new landscape you're stepping into look like?

How do you feel crossing this threshold?

What are you choosing to leave behind?

What are you choosing to take with you to support you on the journey ahead?

Close your eyes for a few moments now and visualise yourself taking this step. Feel the sensations in your body as you do this.

You're on your way, unbound one.

UNBOUND WRITING ACTIVATION

How can I commit more fully to my book writing journey?
What is one action I could take right now to show this commitment?

STAGE TWO: *Conceive*

The second stage of unbound writing is to conceive the idea for your book. So, what specifically do I mean by that?

Some definitions of conceive are:

to become pregnant

to form or devise a plan or idea in the mind

to form a mental representation of: imagine

to become affected by (a feeling)

When we consider conceiving an idea, many of us will think about this as a mental process. Surely you just need to sit at your desk with your laptop or notebook and figure out what to write about?

Hmmm, nope!

This is NOT going to do the trick when it comes to unbound writing. Your unbound book is not going to come from a place of logic or 'figuring it out', however comforting that idea might feel.

Unbound writing lends itself to the first definition of conceive: to become pregnant. You want to become pregnant with your idea. And this demands certain conditions.

When I first started my business, I had a hypnotherapy practice and one of the areas I specialised in was fertility. I helped women who were trying to get pregnant to create the perfect conditions, both consciously and unconsciously, in order to conceive.

This work was incredibly rewarding and I LOVED receiving messages with pictures of the babies who had been born to the women I worked with. And the work was also incredibly challenging. Many of these women had been wanting to have a baby for years, so by the time they came to see me they were very much in 'trying' mode. The very act of 'trying' suggests effort, exertion, the overriding desire to 'make' something happen. This in itself can lead to resistance that gets in the way of creating the desired outcome. So, my job was to help the women I was working with to find ways to relax, to joyfully anticipate the baby they were creating (whilst also acknowledging any natural fears and doubts that might arise), to have a pleasureful relationship with the masculine and to make space for the magic to happen.

It was a balancing act! The process was full of paradoxes and demanded that the woman involved was able to sit with both uncertainty and knowing, fear and hope, relaxation and determination.

What I realise now is that the same applies when it comes to the conception of any creative project, including writing a book.

Rather than trying, pushing and striving to force your book into existence, the ideal conditions for conception are a relaxed space (where there's also the possibility of a breathless quicky!), to work in alignment with your cyclical nature, to joyfully merge the masculine and feminine AND to be ready for magic.

When you're conceiving the idea for your book, you need to be able to stay deeply connected to the excitement and passion of your vision, whilst acknowledging any fears, doubts or old stories that may arise.

You need to allow it ALL. And that's not always (or ever!) easy. But I've got your back, unbound one. So, let's dive into this some more.

On the importance of trust

One of the main challenges that can come up before you even start writing your book is the question of what to actually write about. So many people get stuck at this stage.

What's the right thing to focus on?

And the reason this can feel so completely paralysing is the idea that there's a 'right' thing to be focusing on in your writing. And that if you don't find that thing, then what's the point?

Well, allow me to let you into a secret - there is no elusive right thing for you to be focusing on in your writing. You get to choose whatever you want to write about.

'Eh? What do you say Nicola? I thought a big part of your message (and this book) is about connecting with the specific ideas that want to come through me at this time?'

Well, yes, that's right. I love to open up readers to the possibility that book ideas are active partners in the writing process and that the whole thing can be a joyful collaboration.

BUT, I don't ever want that to become another way you keep yourself stuck.

Must

Find

The

Right

Thing.

No! The most vital thing, above all, is that you get to express your unique voice, your unique energy, your unique essence in the world. And really, you could choose ANYTHING, any subject matter as a way to channel that.

Just decide. Decide what you want to write about and begin. Start with the intention of being fully expressed. And you can't go wrong with that.

Because when you begin with the pure and powerful intention of being fully expressed you get to bypass all of the soul-sucking, creativity sapping questions, like:

'What should I write about?'

'Do I know enough?'

'Am I a good enough writer?'

I mean, wtaf? This idea that there's some exclusive club that you have to be a member of to class yourself as a writer? That there's some special way, some specific rules that you need to follow in order to write a book?

That's all BS.

Because let's get back to basics - what is a book?

In its simplest form, a book is simply a way of communicating a message or a story (or both) in written form.

Now I'm pretty sure you're already doing that in one way or another - maybe via a blog or social media posts or even just messaging your friends. And you're sure as hell doing it verbally. You communicate your message and your stories every freaking day.

And I'm sure you're pretty damn amazing at this when you get out of your own way and give yourself permission to write or talk freely. You know when you're sharing something for the joy of it? When you can't NOT share it? When there's something you're particularly passionate or excited about.

When you're with friends and you want them to know something.

Imagine if you allowed yourself to channel that quality into your writing and onto the page?

Why not go ahead and do it? Because believe me, unbound one, there is no right way to write a book.

And the reason so many of us can get stuck at the beginning stages is a chronic lack of self-trust.

Maybe you've begun writing before and then after a couple of days or weeks, the doubts have crept in and the words have dried up?

'Who am I to do this? Who am I kidding? I can't write a book!'

Self-trust drains away.

And this is no surprise. Because particularly as women, we're pretty much conditioned not to trust ourselves from our youngest years.

Sitting in the audience at an event in New York City where author Glennon Doyle was speaking, I could feel the truth in her words as she talked about how the patriarchal culture we live in indoctrinates us to mistrust ourselves.

On so many levels and in so many ways, we're taught not to trust our bodies, our choices, our desires and, above all else, our inner knowing.

We're taught to look outside for the answers, that someone else (usually someone in authority) knows better than us.

The message we receive continually, over and over again, is: 'Be careful! Question yourself. Always.'

So, it's no wonder if you haven't been fully trusting yourself to write a book.

Well, fuck that! Look, I'm a writer. I love books and I think they're completely magical. But we can't hold them too seriously. I don't ever want you to write from a place of 'Oh my goodness, I've got to get this right'.

I want to encourage you to say 'Fuck it!' and have some freaking fun.

Allow your soul to play on the page.

Let your inner child have a voice.

Give your Unbound Self the pen.

You.

Can't.

Get.

This.

Wrong.

Imagine if you allowed yourself to truly believe that? That's the feeling I invite you to hold as we move ahead on this journey.

THE book

This stage is all about unlocking, beckoning forward and allowing the book that wants to be birthed through you.

I know that you're an amazing, multifaceted being who could write any number of books, about any number of things. I'm sure you have different things that you're passionate about, different elements of your experience that you could be sharing in your writing. But there's a very specific book that's wanting to come through you at this time (and it's the perfect time for it to come through).

This stage two of conception is about tuning into that very specific book and making space for that to happen. So, like I said, it's about writing THE book, not just any book.

And if you're thinking, 'But Nicola, surely that completely contradicts what you've just said about there not being one right thing to focus on in my book', I get it! There's a paradox here (and as you're an unbound being, I know you can hold a paradox). I want you to know that yes, there is a particular book that's wanting to be birthed through at this time and also that the way you get to connect with that is through playing, starting to write (about whatever calls), and trusting that following your breadcrumbs of inspiration will lead you where you need to go.

Now I've mentioned before that we move backwards and forwards between these stages. So, certainly with conceiving your book, you will get ideas coming through at the beginning of the process, and I'm sure that's been happening for you already. But know that this will continue to evolve throughout the process. You want to leave space for magic to happen. You want to leave space for a process of evolution, gaining new insights into what you want to share in your writing as you go, moving deeper on your own, unique journey. So this stage is about connecting to that initial spark of an idea and then providing the fuel for it to grow.

You don't wait for clarity. You write for clarity.

As I've shared with you already, this happened with both of my books. I started out with an idea and both ended up being something quite different, particularly with UNBOUND (*well, it would, wouldn't it? Because... unbound!*). You want to trust that process, so you're conceiving your book all the way through your writing, right up until the end.

On creative collaboration

One of the challenges you might have been experiencing up until now is either having NO clue what to write about or having so many ideas that you get confused and end up procrastinating.

The good news is that there's a way of moving beyond these challenges. There really is a specific book that's waiting to come through you right now and it has a unique essence of its own. And you can choose to connect with that book, gain insights from it and ask questions.

The unbound writing journey isn't meant to be a solitary process where you have to figure everything out on your own.

This journey can be a creative collaboration between you, your book and your Unbound Self.

In the free bonus resources for this book, you can access a short visualisation designed to help you connect with your book and gain powerful insights into what you're here to write about at this time. Listening to this will help you to bypass any doubt and connect with a clear sense of purpose in your writing. You'll move from trying to figure it out to a place of KNOWING.

Sound good? I know this might feel a bit different from any approach to writing you've tried before, but believe me, it's powerful. I receive messages time and time again from writers who have found this Connecting With Your Book Visualisation incredibly helpful.

Go take a listen at: nicolahumber.com/connecting-with-your-book-visualisation

Conditions for conceiving

This stage also involves thinking about the ideal conditions for conceiving your book idea.

What qualities help you feel inspired? How can you create space for your ideas to come through? What helps you to be in a place of receptivity?

For me personally, it's when I'm in nature that I'm really able to connect with and conceive the ideas that want to come through me. Maybe it's the same for you? Or perhaps there's another time or place when you feel most connected to your creative muse?

Space is really important here; having a sense of spaciousness, and cultivating that in whatever way you can. It doesn't have to be a huge amount of space, but just having some time during your day where you're free of distractions or busyness, and you can just really connect with your book.

So, take some time now to journal on the question:

What are the conditions that I need to create in order to conceive my book, the book that wants to come through me?

See what comes up and decide how you can put this in place.

UNBOUND WRITING ACTIVATION

What is the idea that my book is wanting to express through me right now?

STAGE THREE: *Create*

Stage three is create - to actually write your book. As I've been saying, you don't need to wait to create, you want to start creating even before you're clear exactly where you're going in your writing.

Just begin.

Allow it to come through you.

And once you've made that initial commitment, know that you've created the container, so you can trust that whatever is coming through is EXACTLY what needs to emerge, even if it doesn't make sense, even if it's not what you thought you'd be writing about.

Once you've made the commitment and you've conceived that initial spark (or sparks) of an idea, you'll start to receive new insights and this can happen in many different ways.

Maybe you'll have a conversation with a friend that relates to what you're writing about?

Perhaps a client will ask you a question that inspires something new to come through for you.

You might read something or see a video that gives you a new perspective you want to explore.

You begin to notice different themes emerging in your experience. The key is to really trust that this is all coming through for a reason, and to follow these breadcrumbs of inspiration, even if they feel divergent or messy and you're not sure where they're taking you.

And this applies to how you write as much as to what you write. Jo Gifford, author of the super-inspiring *Brilliance Unboxed* shares this about her writing process:

Initially I was making space for the book in a way that I had a goal to write a certain amount of words per day. But, because life is how it is, when you have kids and elderly parents who have a lot of illnesses, and you have three chronic illnesses yourself, and you're working, I wasn't hitting those deadlines. So I thought, right, I need to unbox myself from this way of writing, I need to embrace this unbound way. I need to step into accumulating this information in a way that feels really aligned.

I began recording audios in the morning when I was doing my make-up. I would have maybe five or ten minutes before the girls had gone to school, or I'm just doing my wellness routine and self-care stuff. I'd have a thought in my head, and I would just brain-dump it every day. And then I'd send it off to be transcribed. Then every week, I'd have five of these transcripts come back. I didn't look at them, I just kept outputting. Then at the same time, whenever I'd find some space, I would go back to my old blog posts, my old Instagram posts. All of this stuff that I suddenly realised was all incredibly related to this book that was beginning to unfold.'

Interview for the Magical Portal Project, August 2019

How liberating is that? Know that you get to create in your own way, unbound one, a way that works for you. And it doesn't have to look like anyone else's process.

In this section, I'm going to help you to both have a writing practice that feels good for you AND start to create a fluid map for your book and what you're going to be writing about.

The power of not knowing and not doing

Can you trust that you're being guided in some way, even when your process feels uncertain?

The truth is, it's important (and a key skill of being unbound) to allow unknowing. You allow yourself to move forwards even though you don't know exactly where you're heading. And sometimes you may feel like there's nothing coming through, and you're in this void-like place where it feels like you can't actively create at all. And that's all good. Know that this is also part of the process, because very often there's stuff going on under the surface.

Contrary to what you might have learned in the past, creation isn't always about actively writing and doing. The creative process needs periods of space; time to just be and allow your ideas to bubble away out of your conscious awareness.

This can feel uncomfortable, because we're conditioned to DO. And if you've told yourself (and others) that you're writing a book and suddenly you're not actively doing, you can begin to question yourself and your process.

'Have I lost it?'

'Am I just kidding myself?'

'What if I never have an idea or creative impulse ever again?'

Please know that these are likely to be some of your most powerful times. Those periods of not knowing; time spent in the void.

The key is to notice whether you're dwelling in the void out of fear and procrastination, rather than as a part of your creative process, and that's something that comes through time as you build your awareness.

Divine Discipline

When you're in this creation stage, you (obviously!) want to prioritise your writing. But how can you do this in a way that stills feel free? When I'm working with my unbound writing clients, we talk about the practice of divine discipline. Now, because you're unbound, it's more than likely you'll resist structure and having any sort of a rigid plan, but there is a way of invoking the power of discipline whilst maintaining a sense of expansiveness and freedom. Divine discipline is where we choose to see discipline as a way of being in service to something greater.

Your 'something greater' could be your vision, your desire to be in service God, the Goddess, Mother Earth, your ancestors, Source, your Higher Self. It doesn't matter exactly what you write in service to, what matters is that it's something that allows you to connect with a sense of dedication, devotion; something that activates you to bring discipline into your writing practice.

This is all about balancing the ebbs and flows of your cyclical nature with the desire to to show commitment to your writing practice and complete your book. It's a process of experimentation. Some weeks you might feel like you've nailed it. Others you may feel that you've swung too far one way or the other. That's absolutely fine, unbound one. You'll learn more about what works for you (and what doesn't) as you go.

To get you started with the idea of divine discipline, I invite you to reflect on these questions:

1. What or who am I choosing to dedicate my writing practice to?

2. How can I see my writing practice as serving something greater?

3. What can I put in place to bring a sense of Divine Discipline into my writing?

4. How can I show a greater sense of commitment and dedication to my writing?

Notice what comes up for you as you answer these questions. As ever, the answers will be unique to you and you can experiment with different ways of bringing Divine Discipline into your writing practice.

Your Reader's Journey

To help create a clear and potent structure for your book, I want you to think about the journey you will take your reader on.

A key part of the unbound writing process is to activate transformation in your readers, to create a space where they can experience a sense of movement, from one state to another.

This is powerful and it's immensely helpful for you to be really intentional about how you do this.

So, take some time to journal on the following questions:

1. What's the journey I want to take my reader on as they read this book?

2. Where is my reader at the beginning of the process? How are they likely to be feeling when they come to my book? What kind of experiences are they likely to have been having?

3. What challenges or resistance might my reader be experiencing? How can I help them to move through them with my book? What resources/tips/strategies/stories could I include?

4. What are the signposts I can include along the way as my reader moves through my book? How can I guide them clearly through this process? What do I want them to know? How do I want my reader to feel as they come to the end of the book? What do I want to leave them with? How can I help them to feel supported on their onward journey?

As with everything in the unbound writing process, you can't get this wrong. Just write down whatever wants to come through. *You might like to take yourself out for a walk or some other form of movement whilst reflecting on these questions. That can help ideas to come through you.*

Once you have your answers, you can start to put together a plan for your book which reflects the journey you want to take your reader on. You can imagine this as a map. *You may actually like to draw it out as a map - get as creative as you like!*

Notice how you feel to have this plan and this clear sense of your reader's journey. Is there anything that's missing? Does it feel like you need to include anything else to help your reader get from one place to another?

Is there anything that feels like it's NOT needed at this stage?

Know that this plan, this map, can change and grow and evolve.

Your Story

Another key aspect of the unbound writing process is to bring yourself and your stories into the book you're writing.

It can be tempting to hide behind your expertise and knowledge (*of which I KNOW you have a lot!*), but the one thing that will make your book unique and truly compelling to your soul-family readers is YOU.

We want to hear your stories, we want to hear how you've got to where you are today and what makes you so passionate about whatever it is you're choosing to write.

I invite you to reflect on your own personal stories that you want to include in the book. These are what will bring your book to life! To help with this, take some time to journal on the following questions:

1. What are the key turning points that have brought me to where I am now?

2. What experiences from my childhood feel like they shaped the way I see the world?

3. When were the times in my life that I felt completely lost and how did I find my way?

4. What is the story that I'm secretly scared to tell?

5. What experiences have I had over the past year that feel relevant to my book?

6. What are the stories that I always end up telling and that people love to hear?

7. When I look back, what feel like the most magical experiences of my life?

8. When I think about my book, what is the story that immediately comes to mind?

At this stage, simply write a list of all the stories and experiences that come through as you reflect on these questions. Again, you might like to take yourself for a walk or connect with the essence of your book in some other way as you spend time with these questions.

Once you have your list, go back to the plan/map you created in the previous section. Start to place your individual stories wherever you feel they sit best.

Know that this is not set in stone! You can change it as you go. The idea here is to get a sense of the personal stories and experiences you want to include in your book.

It's also likely that you'll have experiences during the writing process that are relevant to what you're sharing in your book. Look out for these and take some time to write about them as you go.

When you have this list of your personal stories and experiences, you can then use them as an anchor for your writing practice. As I've shared, the unbound writing process is often most powerful when we give ourselves permission to write in a non-linear way. But sometimes this can feel messy and disjointed. This list will give you something to come back to and tune into, 'what do I want to write about today?' You can pick one story or experience from your list and write about that, knowing that you're making progress and working within the fluid structure you've created for your book.

Intentional Writing Practice

I want to help you create a personal writing practice that feels amazing for you AND allows you to write your book in the most potent way.

Part of this is being really intentional about your writing practice and the qualities you want to infuse it with. To help with this, I invite you to reflect on these two questions:

1) How do I want to feel as I write my book?

2) How do I want my reader to feel as they read my book?

Take some time to jot down the feelings that come to mind. It's likely that there will be at least some crossover between how you want to feel and how you want your reader to feel.

When you have a list of feelings, focus on the three that feel most compelling and ask yourself:

How can I infuse my writing practice with these qualities?

See what ideas come to mind.

For example, if one of the feelings that came through for you was FREE, you might choose to write outdoors in nature or perhaps you could have a dance break before sitting down to write?

If one of your feelings is INSPIRED, you could go to an art gallery before writing, or listen to a talk by someone who inspires you.

If one of your feelings is BOLD, you might choose to write in an outfit that makes you feel this way, or listen to some music that has that effect?

You get the idea. Have fun and play with this. Experiment with different ways of infusing your writing practice with the qualities you want to bring through in your book and see what works for you.

Being intentional about how you want to feel during your writing practice is deceptively powerful. On a call with unbound writer Tonia Gaudiuso, she said she had been feeling frustrated that she was struggling to complete a section of her book. Tonia's book, *The New Commodities*, is all about creating a more expansive relationship with money and in it, she takes you through a powerful step-by-step process to do just that. Things had been going so well; the previous week she'd been spending four hours a day writing, but now it felt like she'd hit a wall.

As we were talking, Tonia had a lightbulb moment. The section she was working on now was Flow, which is all about (of course) being in flow and allowing yourself to be playful. The trouble was, she'd been approaching this in the same way as the previous sections that were more practical and detail-focused. What Tonia realised she needed to do was write in a way that allowed her to flow - spending time in nature, coming back to her personal reiki practice and writing in a gentler way.

At different times, you'll want to bring different energies in your writing. So be intentional about how you do that.

Out the doubts

As I shared earlier in the book, one of the layers of unbound writing is allowing the alchemy of shadow integration. And this certainly comes into play during this Create stage.

It's very likely that as you move more deeply into your writing process all sorts of stuff will bubble to the surface. By 'stuff' I very much mean all of the fears and doubts that can make you question why you even started to write a book in the first place. *I mean, what were you thinking?!*

Well, rather than pushing these old stories and beliefs away, or allowing them to make you feel wrong in some way, I instead invite you to WELCOME them.

Now this might have you thinking, '*What?? Nicola, I just want to shove all of this stuff as far away as possible!*'

And I get that.

But as we've been talking about, unbound writing is a transformational process. Rather than choosing to push our 'stuff' away, (or ignore it altogether) we transmute it into the gold of truly compelling writing.

So, how does this work exactly?

Well, when it comes to writing the book you're REALLY here to write, you need to be writing from the fullest expression of who you are.

And this means acknowledging anything you've previously pushed away into the shadows: the 'I'm not good enough', 'Who would want to read what I have to share?', 'Who am I to write a book?' fears, doubts and restrictive stories.

We bring them out into the open and simply acknowledge them as a completely normal part of being a human being who is expanding into her multi-faceted most magnificent, unbound self. *Believe me, EVERYONE experiences the same kind of fears and doubts when it comes to sharing their magic with the world.*

This simple acknowledgement is the first step to moving beyond your 'stuff' and also creating a deeper connection with your readers. Because believe me, if something is coming up for you, it's very likely it's coming up for anyone who's reading your book as well in some way.

So, let's start this process now. Take some time to ask the question: What are the thoughts and feelings that have been holding me back from writing my book up until now?

Write down whatever comes up, without censoring yourself or trying to justify what bubbles up. Give yourself at least 10 minutes for this. Whenever you feel yourself stopping, ask the question, 'And what else?'

When you've done this, take some time to look at what you've written. Aim for an attitude of playful curiosity as you do this.

How do you feel to allow space for these thoughts and feelings that maybe you've tried to push away in the past?

Bring it to the page

If you feel that you're getting stuck because of these fears, doubts or repetitive thoughts, a powerful way to move through this is to bring them to the page. Whether you're writing your book in a notebook or on your laptop, bring whatever is coming up for you there. Write it down and acknowledge it. For example, maybe you'll write something like this:

'Right now, as I sit down to write, I'm really feeling like I'm a fraud to even think about writing a book.'

Notice how it feels to acknowledge this on the page. You're likely to experience a sense of spaciousness and liberation simply by doing this.

Then take it a step further by reflecting on these questions. There are quite a few, so choose those that call to you most:

'What's underneath this doubt/fear?'

'Where in my body am I aware of this doubt/fear?'

'What is this fear/doubt wanting to tell me?'

'When have I felt like this before?'

'When did I first experience this doubt/fear?'

'Whose voice is speaking to me when I hear that doubt/fear in my mind?'

'What is this fear/doubt REALLY about?'

'How would my Unbound Self respond to this fear/doubt?'

'How am I choosing to respond to this fear/doubt?'

Notice how you feel different after doing this. Freer and more expansive, right?

As I've said, the magical thing about this is that if this stuff is coming up for you, it's very likely it will be coming up for your reader in some way. So everything you've just allowed through by bringing this to the page and diving into those self-reflective questions will be really great material for your book. #winwin.

Our fears and doubts thrive in the shadows. When you bring them to the page and acknowledge what's coming up, you allow them to be released. I promise, as soon as you start to do this, it will create a shift.

You start to see your 'stuff' from a different perspective.

You see how these fears and doubts can actually bring something really powerful to your book, adding another layer to your writing, whilst helping you to move beyond what's coming up? It's like magic!

When I guide writers through this process in the Unbound Book Lab, they often find it surprisingly liberating. Although there can be some initial resistance to inviting your fears and doubts forwards, it can help you to see just how absurd many of them are. Allowing this stuff into the open can help to neutralise it; our fears lose their power once we acknowledge them.

So, let's move towards one of the main doubts that can come up when you're thinking about writing a book.

Who am I to?

One of the most common doubts that can come up when we start writing a book and think about sharing it with the world is the question, *'Who am I to do this?'*

The 'Who am I to?' question has probably come up MANY times during your life and I can pretty much guarantee that it will come up at least once during your book-writing journey. So, let's turn it on its head!

Rather than letting this stop you, I invite you to take this question on and write down all the ways you ARE the perfect person to be writing your particular book.

Write down all the experience you have (formal and informal), why you're passionate about your book, what has brought you to this point.

Write about all the ways you've 'failed' in your life, the challenges you've experienced and how you've moved through them.

Write about the lessons you've learned along the way and the kind of reader you now want to share them with.

Consciously prove your doubts wrong!

Once you've done this, take some time to look back at what you've written. Whenever you notice fears or doubts coming up during your book-writing journey, you can come back to this 'Who am I to? prompt and anchor yourself back into the fact that you are the PERFECT person to be writing your book.

UNBOUND WRITING ACTIVATION

*How does it feel to acknowledge that I am absolutely
the perfect person to be writing my book?*

STAGE FOUR: *Community*

Stage four is to create community around your writing. This is about seeing the bigger vision for your book and realising that it can be so much more than just a book.

Your book has the potential to start a movement.

Your book can become a foundation for other offerings you may be inspired to create, and for sharing your magic in different ways - retreats, workshops, programs, membership communities, one-to-one work or speaking opportunities.

There are a multitude of ways for you to create community around your book and, as I've been sharing, I'm a strong believer in the idea that you don't have to wait until your book is out there to start doing just that. You can start creating community right NOW, whether you're at the beginning of your writing process or a bit further in.

I encourage you to share your writing as you go. You can share small pieces of your writing as social media posts, create blog posts, make videos, do Facebook lives, run programs or workshops or retreats based on what's coming through in your writing process. You don't have to wait. And in fact, sharing as you go gives you powerful information and inspiration to take back into the creation stage and the conception stage. You'll get the most gorgeously rich ideas from interacting with other people around your writing, rather than choosing to do it in isolation.

When I wrote my second book, *UNBOUND*, I was sharing pieces of it all the way along, and it became a dynamic process between myself and the community that I was creating around my writing. Doing this helps you to anchor into your book and your work in the most magical way, because you're inviting people into your process, you're allowing them to share in it, to be part of it. And for me now, *UNBOUND* really does feel like a movement because I allowed other people into this journey long before my book was actually out there in the world. And it's now given birth to this whole other area of work around writing and books, which is another aspect of this movement.

Can I let you into a secret?

Your book is more than a book. It's more than a collection of pages for someone to read.

With your book you're writing new ways into the world. You're creating a vision for something important, something unique, something needed.

You're creating a movement (whether you want to or not).

You're activating change, evolution, growth.

You're shifting paradigms.

You're sharing a vision of how things can be different and inviting people to come with you.

When you open up to thinking about and feeling into your book in that way, you become unstoppable.

When you're deeply connected to your vision, you can't help but write your book.

This is what strengthens your container and keeps you going.

What is your vision for the world?

What aspect of life are you writing about and inviting your vision forward into?

Take some time to reflect on these questions now. Allow yourself to get excited. Only you can do this. You might not believe that quite yet, but as I've been saying, each of us has our own unique chord to add to the orchestra of this world. If you're not contributing, it won't sound the same. Something will be off, flat, missing.

Your part, your vision, is necessary. Please don't deprive us of it. Allow yourself to thrive through this process. Part of that is inviting sisterhood and support as you write. And also creating community around your writing. On which note...

Glow

Something that comes up when we're thinking about writing a book is a desire to reach as many people as possible with it. There's so much hype about best-seller lists and all that jazz. It can feel like a huge pressure to reach a wider audience.

I've felt like that too. I want my writing and my work to reach as many people as possible. I'm passionate about the unbound message. I don't want anyone to be living in a way where they're feeling trapped by 'shoulds'. And if you're reading this book, I'm guessing you're just as passionate about your message.

But... we want to use that passion as fuel rather than experiencing it as a pressure to reach ALL of the people. The unbound way isn't about pushing and striving and hustling.

The unbound way is underpinned with kindness, to yourself and others. I don't want you to feel that you have to stretch yourself paper-thin to do all the things.

So, let me suggest a way to think about your audience, your community, your sisterhood, differently. You want to reach a lot of people with your book and have a powerful impact, right?

Great! I'm over here cheering you on and here's how I want you to imagine creating that.

I invite you to imagine, know, visualise that your book is like a glowing log, a beautiful campfire. It radiates a powerful warmth and its light attracts people (your readers) closer.

As your readers come close to the glow, something is activated within them and their own glow ignites. They then take this glow, this warmth, this light, with them and it brings others closer. The sense of activation, the igniting power of your book, ripples out from person to person.

You don't have to radiate that heat to the furthest edges of your audience. You simply focus on nurturing the glow and allowing it to entrance, intrigue, activate those who come closer to you.

Your readers carry the flame and pass it on from one to another.

But will they get it?

So this community stage is very important, but it's one we can resist because you might be thinking, *'Oh, I'm not sure if other people will get this, or will they really be interested?'* All of these questions come up. And do you know what, unbound one? Those questions will continue to come up until you allow yourself to share your writing, so I encourage you to do it. If you wait until the book is written to share it, it's going to feel much bigger, whereas if you share it as you go, you're receiving feedback throughout the process. And when you're following this unbound writing process, then I can pretty much guarantee you're going to get amazing feedback for your writing, because you're writing in this super-compelling way.

So I invite you to think, what kind of community do you want to create around your writing? Start to get excited about that. This can really help to carry you through, and it ties back in with the commitment stage because you're not just making that commitment for yourself, you're making it for the community that you want to grow around your writing.

Intentional community

Your book has a life of its own and as you continue on your writing journey, it will begin to go out into the world creating a unique relationship with each of the people it comes into contact with.

You can't control how each reader experiences your book - each person will take something different and that is a truly magical thing.

But you can be intentional about the community you want to create around your book.

As we've been talking about here, as you write your book and release it into the world, you have the opportunity to create a movement, a community of people who have similar challenges, intentions and desires.

You have the opportunity to bring people together around your writing.

When we come together, we become more.

And creating an intentional community around your book will increase the potency of the message you're here to share.

So, let's take some time to think about the kind of community you want to create.

Who is your book for?

What is the vision you hold for the people who choose to read your book?

What qualities do you want to infuse into the community you're creating around your writing?

What is the main focus of your community?

How will people benefit from being part of it?

How do you want to connect with and grow your community? Is there a particular social media platform that feels good for you? An email list? In-person meet-ups or online gatherings? (*Please know that you can choose to use any or all of these options. The aim is to be powerfully intentional and choose the ways that feel unbound for you, because your community will FEEL that*).

Once you've taken some time to journal on the above questions, ask yourself:

'What's the first step I could take right now towards creating or growing my community?'

Go do it.

UNBOUND WRITING ACTIVATION

What kind of community do I feel called to create around my writing? Imagine that you're writing a manifesto for the most unbound vision of what you want your community to experience. Share your values, dreams, hopes and desires for the work you're here to do and those who are going to connect with this.

ON FINISHING YOUR BOOK

So, you've been working on your book, allowing what wants to come through to come. You've made progress. And your thoughts start to turn to how you'll actually complete the process.

How will you know when your book is finished?

How many words should it be?

And how on earth do you bring it all together? These are all questions that bubble up as we write. And the truth is there's no one right answer.

People often ask me how many words their book should be and I can understand the desire to have a particular number in mind. I remember Googling, 'how long should a non-fiction book be?' when I wrote my first book. I wanted someone to tell me the answer, to give me a number to aim for.

I can't remember what the search results told me. I'm sure there were a range of answers. Because, unbound one, each book needs to be as many words as it takes to express what you want to share. Only you know how many words that will be. And you most likely won't have a sense of that until you're deep in your writing process. At some point you'll feel, 'Ah I see. This book feels like it's going to be around _____ words'. For me, each of my books has been around 30000 words. That hasn't been planned; they've just all felt done at that point. The Unbound Press books that have been released so far have ranged between 16,000 and 100,000 words plus, so you can see how this varies.

As you come to the end of writing your book, you'll feel when it's complete. And complete is different to perfect. Your book will probably never feel perfect. (If it does, then go you!) But you'll reach a point where it feels done, where it's good enough. That's the point where you get to go through your first draft, make any changes, add anything that needs to be added, lose anything that feels unnecessary and see that it flows well (if you're not working with a publisher, you can hire an editor to help you with this).

Trust that when your book feels 'cooked', it's done. You could faff and fiddle around with it forever, but the most important thing is that it gets to go out into the world.

Very often new insights about the structure and content of your book will drop in towards the end of the process. The unbound way means that you're only given whatever you need at any particular time. Your book, your guides, the big U, will surprise you with new awarenesses about your writing at every stage of your journey. Trust that. And know that you are deeply supported in your process. Always.

Finishing a book is certainly not my favourite part of the process. I love the beginning, the excitement of a brand new adventure, fresh ideas and a blank page. The nitty gritty finishing touches of the ending can feel painful for me quite frankly. I liken it to the actual birth process, (not that I've experienced that personally, but using my imagination here!). You've had the pleasure of conception, the joy of announcing you're expecting a (book) baby, the intimate experience of carrying your creation within you. Now it needs to come out. 'Hmmm, did I really sign up for this?' You want to meet your (book) baby. You want it to be out in the world. But the actual birthing? Can someone else do that bit?

I had a big shift around this when I heard Sheila Kay talking about Ecstatic Birth at the same time I was completing *UNBOUND*. I'd been grumbling about these end stages, telling myself and anyone who would listen, 'I hate this part of writing a book'. But hearing Sheila talk about birth in this completely different way prompted me to ask: 'What if I chose to enjoy this part of the process, to take pleasure, to feel the ecstasy of birthing?'

Since then it's not always been an ecstatic process, but I can see and feel the pleasure in completion, the exquisite release of birthing.

And when your book goes out into the world? There's no better feeling. Yes, we can have all the familiar fears and doubts bubbling up:

What will people think?

What if no-one gets it?

What if I get a one-star review?

But, the fact is, you've written a book.

Most people don't get to do that. Many think about it, many dream of being an author, many say, 'I know I've got a book in me', but very few complete the process.

This is my wish for you, unbound one, that you will write and finish your book (and then the next one, and the next one), that it will go out into the world and the impact will ripple out through your readers, through the collective, through you.

Thank you for holding this dream in your heart.

Thank you for being a magical being who has something so important to share with the world.

Thank you for being an unbound writer.

BOOK BLESSING

I now activate this book's journey into the world.

I know that each book is a vital piece of a larger whole.

With this book I bring through and welcome new ways into the world.

May this book reach the people it's meant to reach.

May this book activate the most powerful and magical transformation both in myself as the author and each of its readers.

May this book find it's own unique way to make the impact it's here to make, for the highest good.

May this book be infused with love, peace and abundant blessings.

I thank my guides on this unbound writing journey, my unbound sisters around the globe and the essence that wants to be expressed through me at this time.

I give thanks for this mysterious and magical journey I'm on.

I honour the writer I'm here to be and this book as the vessel of my unique medicine.

I bless this book and all who connect with it.

And so it is.

ACKNOWLEDGEMENTS

As I come to the end of writing this book, I want to acknowledge and thank the following people who have all played a part in supporting and inspiring me on this journey:

To my Dad, who has now passed on, thanks for putting money aside to buy books for us when we were little and starting my love for them.

To Mum, thanks for being there, always.

To Lou, thanks for being my sister on this soul path. You inspire me SO much.

To Mark, thank you for being my Mr H, cheering me on and walking by side as we adventure together.

To Tonia, thank you for being the fiercest, most fabulous Sister Goddess there is. I'm so glad we got to go on this unbound writing journey together.

To Sean Patrick and Clare Roche, who both guided me onto this unbound writing path.

To all the members of the unbound writing family who inspire me every day: Anna Sansom, Jennifer Booker, Tara Jackson, Erica Walther, Sarah Lloyd, Angie Northwood, Jo Gifford, Tonia G, Jessy Paston, Ali Roe, Jacqui McGinn, Sarika Jain, Allyson Ross-Collings, Emma-Louise Smith, Helen Rebello, Amy Babiarz, Sarah Coxon, Pearl Jordan, Isobel Gatherer, Dainei

Tracy, Lorraine Pannetier, Trudi Remer and many more to come. What a magical bunch you are!

ABOUT THE AUTHOR
AND FURTHER RESOURCES

Nicola Humber is the author of two previous transformational books, Heal Your Inner Good Girl and UNBOUND. She's also the founder of The Unbound Press, a soul-led publishing imprint for unbound women.

After playing the archetypal good girl up until her mid-thirties, Nicola left her 'proper' job in finance to retrain as a coach and hypnotherapist and this leap of faith led her to what she does now: activating recovering good girls to embrace their so-called imperfections and shake off the tyranny of 'shoulds', so they can be their fullest, freest, most magnificent selves.

Nicola helps women to write the book their Unbound Self is calling them to write, whilst growing a community of soul-family readers and clients. She's originally from Southampton in the UK, but is now based in upstate New York.

Find out more at: *nicolahumber.com*

Access free Unbound Writing resources at: *nicolahumber.com/unbound-writing-resources*